THE PREPPER'S SURVIVAL BIBLE

13 IN 1

FACE THE APOCALYPSE & SURVIVE SOCIETY'S COLLAPSE, SHELTERED & OFF-GRID. THE DETAILED & ULTIMATE GUIDE TO PROTECTING YOUR FAMILY IN THE WORST-CASE SCENARIO

TABLE OF CONTENTS

BOOK 1: INTRODUCTION TO DISASTER

Readiness has a significant effect because it can save lives in a real sense. Nobody gets a kick out of the chance to contemplate disasters influencing our networks. Whether it's tropical storms, fire outbreaks, earthquakes, or other disasters, examining it is precisely what we need to do.

Kids and families can plan together. Disasters can be scary, but being prepared is one method for being less apprehensive!

SETTING UP YOUR LOVED ONES

Here are a few essential and significant things you can do with your loved ones:

- Discuss with your youngsters about disasters that could occur — and what they should do in case of disaster.
- Know where to get dependable news and data about climate and disasters. Organize at least one or two methods for getting alarms, like texts.
- Train youngsters on the fundamentals of what to do in case of fire outbreaks, for example, bending down to abstain from smoke or feeling the door handles for heat before opening them. Have an emergency exit plan.
- If you live in a space impacted by typhoons, twisters, fierce blazes, or seismic tremors, enlighten the kids about perceiving the signs and where they should go.
- Ensure kids know how to call 911 and can address them. Even exceptionally small kids can know how to do this.
- Settle on an individual (preferably not a neighborhood individual who may be impacted by a similar disaster) that everybody can contact if you are isolated.
- Have a gathering place outside the house where relatives can go if you are isolated and can't find one another.

The COVID-19 pandemic has shown us generally numerous things. It has particularly shown us how rapidly life can change and how useless your pay can be.

As characterized by the United Nations, disaster is a serious disturbance of the functionality of a community or society, which includes inescapable human, material, monetary or natural effects that surpass the capacity of the impacted community or society to adapt by utilizing its own assets. Disaster management is how we manage the human, material, monetary or natural effects of said disaster; it is the course of how we "plan for, answer and gain from the impacts of significant disappointments." Though brought about ordinarily, disasters can have human sources. As indicated by the International Federation of Red Cross and Red Crescent Societies, a disaster happens when a peril influences weak individuals. The mix of dangers, weakness, and failure to lessen the expected adverse results of risk brings about disaster.

Disaster is an extreme worry for the living. Natural disasters and furnished struggle have stamped human presence from the beginning of time and have consistently caused many mortality and grimness. The effect of a disaster can differ from small to great, depending on its sort. Specifically, disasters can have many causes. However, generally speaking, disasters can harm material assets as well as life. Although they are flighty and can be unlimited, there can be many purposes behind which we are additionally dependable.

Before examining the different sorts of disasters, let us see momentarily about the disaster with the help of its definition:

WHAT IS DISASTER?

A disaster is a severe crisis coming about by different vulnerabilities like death, wounds, sickness, and property harm, and frequently not taken care of with routine systems and assets. Such vulnerability can happen in light of multiple factors. The causes can be natural, human mistakes, hardware breakdown, sickness, biological risk, etc.

These disturbances brought about by different disasters can harm human assets, financial assets, ecological supplies, and, surprisingly, the existence of various species, including humans. The span of disasters can go from a moment of interruption to 60 minutes, a day, or seven days, and the impacts can go from minor to huge scope. Although any disaster type might happen for a specific period, it will have long-term impacts ordinarily past the impacted society's decent limit.

TYPES OF DISASTERS

There are many kinds of disasters and can take different structures. In any case, all of them can be extensively classified into the accompanying three classifications:

- Natural Disasters
- Man-made or Technological Disasters
- Complex Emergencies

Natural disasters are natural events that happen gradually or quickly and cause prompt broad demolition of human well-being, prompting demise and languishing. These disasters are principally described by factors like their force or size, region of the reach, term, speed of starting, etc. A few biological exercises, like precipitation, can likewise transform into natural disasters when they happen over as far as possible.

Natural disasters are likewise hurtful to natural assets. They frequently cause mass obliteration. Such disasters hurt humans and different species. For instance, a natural disaster far and wide obliterates the climate and death toll for a creature living in space. Additionally, it harms natural assets and property.

In addition, a few natural disasters might be brought about by different anthropogenic exercises. For instance, deforestation, mining, and horticultural exercises can set off avalanches. Nonetheless, they are classified in the category of natural disasters.

Some common natural disasters are discussed below:

GEOGRAPHICAL DISASTERS

Geographical disasters refer to horrendous events that emerge because of Earth's varieties, either above or underneath the Earth's surface. Specifically, volcanic ejections frequently happen where structural plates connect. Conversely, tremors are inclined to regions with dynamic plate tectonics.

A few normal instances of geographical disasters incorporate tremors, torrential slides, avalanches, tidal waves, sinkholes, volcanic emissions, and so forth.

HYDROLOGICAL DISASTERS

Hydrological disaster refers to quick and vicious events that happen beneath the Earth's surface or in the climate because of varieties in water quality, development, or dissemination. A torrent is a huge section of water or waves essentially brought about by uprooting high measures of water. They are generally brought about by physical exercises under the ocean, like volcanic emissions or seismic tremors.

Some normal instances of hydrological disasters incorporate flooding, tidal waves, limnic emissions, and so on.

Climatological Disasters refer to quick and brutal changes in the world's current circumstances connected with or brought about by the world's environment. It is a danger fundamentally brought about by enduring/meso to large-scale processes ranging from intra-occasional to multi-decadal environment changeability. Additionally, these kinds of disasters can endure from minutes to days. They are additionally classified as Extreme Temperature and Wildfire. Outrageous Temperature events are identified as cool waves, heat waves, and extreme winter circumstances (e.g., icing, torrential slide, snow pressure, freezing precipitation, etc.). Plus, a fierce blaze is identified as the timberland flames and land fires (fires because of grass, scour, etc.).

METEOROLOGICAL DISASTERS

Meteorological disasters are events brought about by outrageous atmospheric conditions, like a downpour, snowfall, or dry spell. Disasters of this kind ordinarily influence the Earth's air and the method for the evolving environment. A few typical instances of meteorological disasters are twisters, hailstorms, and storms. These disasters are highly disastrous to the climate and can devastate many lives, including other species.

BIOLOGICAL DISASTERS

Biological disasters refer to natural and lamentable events that can cause infections, handicaps, or even death at a normal pace for different species, including humans and plants. Biological disasters are characterized as devastating situations brought about by living or non-living creatures that cause a huge scope of extreme sicknesses, infections, or diseases in plants, humans, and different species. These disasters are normally brought about by small organic entities, such as irresistible microorganisms, poisons, infections, etc. A few normal instances of biological disasters incorporate creature maladies and bug-borne infections.

Space disasters are of different sorts. These typically include natural activities in space, like sun-based flares, airburst events, and effect events.

It is likewise said that it caused the termination of all non-avian dinosaurs quite a while back. Sun-oriented flares are characterized as the abrupt arrival of a lot of sun-powered radiation by the sun. Airburst events are seen as the colossal fiery blasts of beams (e.g., Gamma-beam) in far-off worlds. If such an event happens again today, it might bring about many species' mass eradication, including humans.

Disasters can likewise be brought about by humans, either directly or indirectly. Man-made disasters are characterized as the events produced by humans fundamentally in or near human settlements. Such events normally cause ecological or technological emergencies.

Man-made disasters have components of human purpose, carelessness, or mistake that include the man-made framework's disappointment. Furthermore, aggravations in natural assets likewise lead to man-made disasters. The absolute most normal instances of man-made disasters incorporate psychological oppression, huge scope wrongdoing or mass viciousness occurrences, war, pyromania, common turmoil, biological/compound danger, Reduction in the utilization of assets, etc.

Some man-made disasters are examined underneath:

CLIMATE DEGRADATION

Climate corruption is a disaster, including the over-utilization of natural assets, diminishing the climate's capacity to meet social and biological necessities. This, at last, lessens the adequacy of biological system administrations, bringing about the moderation of floods and avalanches. Thus, the risk of natural disasters increases.

CONTAMINATION

Contamination is one more kind of man-made disaster. Although it shows no immediate side effects, it influences natural assets and living creatures. This diminishes the climate's quality and limits the climate's capacity to adjust environmental requirements. From one day to another, contamination arrives at significantly more elevated levels because of humans' huge number of wastes. This prompts expanded risks of disasters. Additionally, when disasters happen, large numbers of them in this manner are dirty and corrupt the climate.

PSYCHOLOGICAL INTIMIDATION

Psychological warfare is a kind of man-made disaster. It is characterized as episodes in which fear mongers use power or viciousness against individuals or property, disregarding criminal regulations for purposes like dangers, disobedience, or payoff. Psychological oppression intends to make agitation within the nation and spread alarm among individuals. Demonstrations of psychological oppression ordinarily incorporate terrorizing, murder, besieging, capturing, abducting, and even digital assaults (acquiring knowledge and security data). Psychological oppressors can likewise utilize synthetic and biological weapons to target individuals at public events, get-togethers, and milestones.

MISHAPS

Mishaps can, in some cases, appear as a disaster. It ordinarily includes unintentional events in which death toll and material are estimated broadly. It includes modern, specialized, and transportation-related mishaps during unsafe materials' creation, use, or transportation.

Disasters can happen because of the effect of numerous disasters. Such disasters are typically classified under complex emergencies. It is, for the most part, characterized as the result of natural and man-made disasters. Specifically, complex emergencies can incorporate the breakdown of power, assaults on essential establishments, plundering, expanding uncontrolled wrongdoings, numerous other struggle circumstances, or even conflicts.

Next is an outline of four kinds of natural disasters.

QUAKES

After a tremor, an emergency clinic is bound to pulverize wounds. If around evening time, many of those wounds will be centered around the pelvis, chest, and legs since numerous casualties will have been set down. Alternately, if the seismic tremor happens during the daytime, the emergency clinic will probably see a convergence of head injury and gashes from broken glass or other material.

FLOODS

In the United States, floods represent more deaths than any remaining disasters on this rundown. An emergency clinic should be prepared to experience casualties that have been presented to the components for extended periods before they could be safeguarded. Hypothermia, injury from falling trash, and slashes are only a couple of the wounds a clinic will experience during a flood.

STORMS

During a storm, a clinic should be prepared to endure the actual typhoon and give clinical consideration to the people in question. In the same way as other disasters, typhoons can cause auxiliary events, such as storm floods, that can be dangerous and give their specific wounds.

Second, to the tempest flood, winds are the second most deadly feature of a typhoon. Wind can send huge articles flying as well as break down structures. Gashes and pound wounds are normal.

TWISTERS:

Since twisters frequently happen with next to zero advance notice, numerous casualties are in structures when they hit. This implies pound wounds are normal. Likewise, standard cut from flying shots, for example, glass or whatever else the breeze gets. If a casualty is found outside during a twister, they will frequently display a scraped spot on their skin from being hit by sped-up components like soil and water. Compound cracks, which have an expanded disease opportunity, are likewise, to some degree, more typical during a cyclone.

These are only a few wounds that can happen during these disasters. Tragically large numbers of the disasters can cause optional disasters, for example, a seismic tremor causing a fire. Clinics should constantly be ready with the devices to give proficient lifesaving care to individuals who need it the most.

SOCIAL POST

Is your medical clinic arranged with each instrument for a natural disaster? Loss of force can mean a death toll. Be ready.

Coming up next are normal attributes for identifying complex emergencies:

- Loss of numerous life
- Broad savagery
- Outrageous harm to economies and social orders
- Removals of populaces
- Expanded security for humanitarian help laborers
- Enormous scope humanitarian guide expected by different offices
- Need for political and military obstructions that affect or prevent humanitarian guide

The absolute most normal sorts of complicated emergencies that fall under the category of disasters are examined beneath:

FOOD INSECURITY

Food instability is typically characterized as an optional sort of disaster. A danger fundamentally implies episodes that cause harm to food stores and food frameworks. For instance, natural disasters, such as floods and dry spells, can harm the farming framework and put away food. Unforeseen environmental changes can likewise influence individuals' food sources. Because individuals need to devour satisfactory, solid, and nutritious food at specific times to carry on with a good life, food weakness prompts issues and different vulnerabilities. Sometimes, it can likewise be because of human activities, like an ineffective investigation of farming.

SCOURGES AND PANDEMICS

The scourge fundamentally includes the overwhelming impacts of disasters brought about by any illness, handicap, or demise of individuals in a specific region or community. Furthermore, pandemics incorporate disasters that influence a huge degree, even the whole nation or the world. For instance, late Covid infection has been proclaimed a pandemic by the WHO (World Health Organization).

DISLODGED POPULATIONS

The dislodged populace includes individuals who have needed to pass on their occupants because of disasters/specialized/deliberate episodes. Individuals can be from similar nations or evacuees (individuals from different nations or inverse lines). This can prompt a specific crisis as there will be vulnerabilities to meet the fundamental primary necessities of jobs. It can compel individuals to carry out wrongdoings and different struggles.

CLASSIFICATION BASED ON CATEGORIES

In its 4.54 long-term history, Earth has encountered different kinds of disasters. A portion of these disasters has prompted many mass eliminations and intense ramifications for different living species. The most widely recognized sorts of disasters can likewise be classified by the accompanying classifications:

WATER AND CLIMATE DISASTERS

This category includes disasters like cold waves, heat waves, hail storms, typhoons, twisters, dry spells, torrents, floods, etc.

GEOGRAPHICAL DISASTERS:

This category includes seismic tremors, cyclones, avalanches, volcanic ejections, etc.

ATOMIC DISASTERS:

This category includes disasters like radiation harming, atomic center implosions, etc.

MAN-MADE DISASTERS:

This category includes disasters like the breakdown of huge structures, fires in metropolitan regions, timberland fires, contamination, etc.

COMPLEX EMERGENCIES

A few disasters can result from numerous dangers or, on a more regular basis, a perplexing blend of natural and man-made causes, including separation of power, plundering and going after essential establishments, struggle circumstances, and war.

These can include:

- Food Insecurity
- Plagues
- Outfitted Conflicts
- Dislodged Populations

As indicated by ICRC, these Complex Emergencies are regularly described by:

- Broad Violence
- Removals of Populations
- Death toll
- Inescapable Damage to both Societies and Economies
- Need for Large-scale, Humanitarian Assistance across Multiple Agencies
- Political and Military Constraints which influence or prevent Humanitarian Assistance
- Expanded Security Risks for Humanitarian Relief Workers
- Pandemic Emergencies

Pandemic is a scourge of irresistible illness that has spread across a vast district, which can happen to the human populace or creature populace and may influence wellbeing and upset administrations prompting monetary and social expenses. It might be a surprising or unforeseen expansion in the number of instances of an irresistible sickness that currently exists in a specific district or populace. It can likewise refer to the presence of a significant number of instances of an irresistible illness in a locale or populace generally liberated from that sickness. Pandemic Emergencies might happen as an outcome of natural or artificial disasters. These have incorporated the accompanying pestilences:

- Ebola
- Zika
- Avian Flu
- Cholera
- Dengue Fever
- Intestinal sickness
- Yellow Fever
- Covid Disease (COVID-19).

Basic instincts are methods an individual might use to support life in a natural or artificial climate. These methods are intended to give necessities to human life, including water, food, and asylum. The abilities likewise support legitimate knowledge and collaborations with creatures and plants to advance the support of life throughout some period. Basic instincts are frequently connected with the need to get by in a disaster. Abilities to survive are, in many cases, essential thoughts and capacities that people of old concocted and involved themselves for millennia. Open-air exercises, for example, climbing, hiking, horseback riding, fishing, and hunting, require fundamental wild abilities to survive, particularly in dealing with crises.

Disasters hit the most unfortunate and the hardest. Destitute individuals are more defenseless against environment-related shocks, yet they have fewer assets to prevent, adapt, and adjust to disasters. The poor generally get less help from the family, community, and monetary frameworks and have less admittance to social wellbeing nets.

This way, disasters can segregate on the same lines that social orders oppress individuals. Disasters will quite often segregate along generational and orientation lines. A few examinations dissecting the effect of disasters have uncovered that ladies and youngsters have more severe risks to their endurance and healing due to natural disasters. The weakness of ladies and kids to natural disasters can be additionally irritated by different components of segregation like race, poverty, and inability.

During the 2017 Hurricane Harvey in the U.S., numerous females — particularly ladies of variety — chose not to clear risk regions regardless of many warnings. Why? From one place to the other, women and young ladies are predominantly entrusted, actually and expertly, focusing on kids, the old, and individuals with handicaps. Thus, straightforward life-saving choices, such as knowing whether to clear a disaster region, can make difficult decisions.

Neediness and orientation standards shape fundamental endurance abilities too. For instance, as per an Oxfam overview, four-fold more women than men were killed in Indonesia, Sri Lanka, and India during the 2004 tidal wave because men were shown how to swim and climb trees at young ages, while women were not.

Admittance to food and nourishing circumstances likewise decide individuals' abilities to adapt to disasters. Kindness Corps reports that ladies and men will generally embrace different strength systems during dry seasons in the Sahel area of Africa — and diminishing food admission is one of them. According to South and Southeast Asia statistics, 45% to 60% of ladies of regenerative age are beneath their normal weight, and 80% of pregnant ladies lack iron. During food deficiencies, ladies are bound to experience the ill effects of lack of healthy sustenance because they have specific wholesome necessities while pregnant or bosom taking care of. Ladies now and again consume fewer calories to give needs to men and kids.

Be that as it may, disasters can likewise shake normal practices and power relations and can offer open doors for progress.

States worldwide progressively perceive the significance of connecting all individuals from networks in disaster risk decrease at public and nearby levels. The World Bank and the Global Facility for Disaster Reduction and Recovery (GFDRR), through the Africa Hydromet Program, are supporting a few African nations to prepare for dry spells and floods. The Africa Hydromet Program commands the consideration of women in specialized fields like meteorology, hydrology, and direction. The program additionally assembles the limit of government authorities to comprehend the orientation aspect of disaster risk decrease.

In Togo, the program will improve public hydro-meteorological and standard assurance administrations. It will likewise grow the Togolese Red Cross' endeavors to engage women's gatherings or clubs des mères (moms' clubs) in expanding community versatility. Agreeing with the Red Cross, remembering people for planning possibility and crisis plans at grassroots levels has saved many lives yet has added to lifting the situation with ladies as problem solvers in their networks.

Present crisis settings tend on be male-overwhelmed; most positions in development and utility restoration are essentially involved by men, so ladies are frequently rejected from the emotional cycle. As UN Volunteers announced on account of the 2016 Ecuador quake, remembering individuals for garbage evacuation and other useful, modern exercises and remaking positions has added to changing orientation generalizations.

How incorporation decreases disaster risks

As per the United Nations, natural dangers have impacted 4.4 billion individuals, guaranteed 1.3 million lives, and caused $2 trillion in financial misfortunes. A natural disaster can stop or oppose progress accomplished over a long time in only a few years. Disasters obliterate resources and lives, yet in addition to earlier advancement endeavors. This includes hard-won advances in orientation correspondence.

Mindfulness impacts how we see natural disasters: females and kids ought to be focal in disaster risk prevention and community strength programs.

At the community level, disaster risk prevention should begin with, young men and young ladies. Youngsters have effectively taken part in planning perils, bringing issues to light through radio and games, and impacting different kids, educators, guardians, and networks on the most proficient method to diminish disaster risks. Examples of overcoming adversity from Indonesia, the Philippines, Vietnam, Thailand, Cambodia, Nepal, and Bangladesh show the effect of including youngsters and youth in disaster risk readiness.

Imbalance and prohibition are man-made disasters on their own; fortunately, they may be switched. Individuals living in neediness are substantially more powerless against the impacts of natural disasters and environmental change, as are underestimated bunches like the least fortunate ladies and kids. Weak individuals can become the most remarkable influencers, and now is an ideal opportunity to roll out this improvement.

BOOK 2: HOW TO PREPARE FOR DISASTERS IN A PRACTICAL WAY

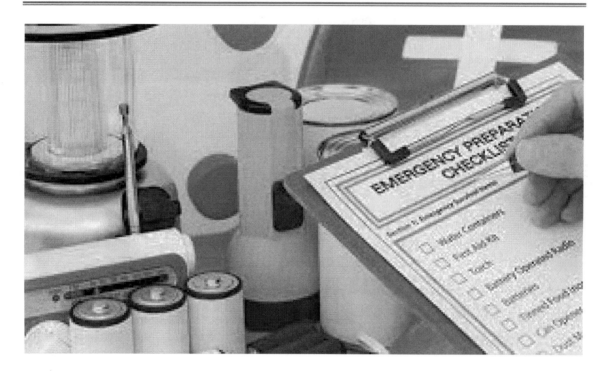

Disasters are unavoidable — eventually, in our lives, we will all have a brush with a quake, flood, cyclone, snowstorm, or tempest. There's no utilization in considering yourself debilitated; a disaster readiness plan is the most effective way to shield yourself against any crisis.

Disaster prevention comes in many ways, from knowing what kind of crisis to expect, pressing a crisis readiness unit to prepare your home, and getting back to it when everything is good. Follow these master obtained disaster readiness tips to guarantee you have a well-thought-out plan set up.

Every emergency requires different planning, supplies, and know-how to some degree. Figure out which disasters your town, state, and locale are most at risk for and plan in like manner. Likewise, really take a look at your home insurance contract to ensure you're secured. While most standard plans cover events like cyclones, lightning, and winter storms, you'll presumably require a different strategy for flooding, windstorms, and quakes.

Quakes: They can occur in all states anytime.

Fierce blazes: High risk in forested regions with a little downpour, like Southern California.

Floods: The most well-known natural disaster can hit any place, particularly in low-lying regions.

Cyclones: "Twister Ally" includes the provinces of TX, OK, IA, KS, NE, and OH, which are on alert from March to August.

Snowstorms: They can happen any place the temperature decreases underneath freezing.

Tempests and Hurricanes: The East and Gulf coasts are at high risk from June to November.

2. PURSUE CRISIS ALARMS.

Get notifications shipped off your telephone from your specialist co-op or through a free application from FEMA or the Red Cross.

3. PACK A "GO SACK."

If you need to leave your home in a rush, you'll need to have a fundamental pressed and all set. Keep the accompanying supplies, suggested by the Federal Emergency Management Agency, in a convenient compartment or "go pack" in the space of your home where you'll take cover.

Survival pack List

- Three days of food and water (essentially a gallon for each relative)
- Battery-controlled (or hand wrench) spotlights and radio
- Additional batteries
- Emergency treatment pack
- Whistle to the flag for help
- Garbage sacks and channel tape, alongside dust veils
- Wrench or pincers to switch off utilities
- Manual can opener for food
- Provincial guides
- Cell with chargers, inverter, or sun-powered charger
- Sodden towelettes and any private disinfection or specific family needs, similar to pet supplies.

We also recommend having more modest variants of your unit supplied with necessities like strolling shoes, durable bites, and a spotlight at work. By and large, you'll likewise require sufficient money available for five days of essential necessities (gas and food), yet any measure of prepared cash will help if ATMs are down.

When you have your provisions together, it pays to go through them something like once a year to get rid of terminated food and batteries.

4. MAKE AN ACTIVITY ARRANGEMENT.

When things get turbulent, you need to ensure that each relative knows what to do. We recommend assigning two gathering places (one nearby and one a little further away in your area) and draping a guide with the spots set apart close to your survival kit.

It additionally pays to have significant contacts down on paper if the power goes out and there's nowhere to charge your mobile phone. Make a smaller contact list with significant numbers that everybody can stash in their wallets. Leave a duplicate in your survival pack, as well. Lay out an arrangement for checking in with family members if neighborhood lines get stuck. Instant messages will frequently go through, even when telephone lines are obstructed.

5. PREP YOUR HOME.

Keep significant reports and papers that would be difficult to supplant fixed in a flame-resistant safe. If you have pets, make a point to incorporate their vet records and their inoculation records; a few vets and pet hotels will not concede your fuzzy family without them. Veterans ought to try to incorporate your DD-214, verifying your confirmation of military assistance. If flooding is normal in your space, put records in a zip-top pack or waterproof holder too.

Significant Documents List

- International IDs
- Birth and reception certificates
- Shot records
- Government-backed retirement cards
- Leases
- Titles
- Deeds
- Wills
- Tenant contracts

If the power goes out, turn off machines and hardware and mood killer climate control systems, whether you stay or go. This will prevent harm when the power floods back on. Leave one light on so you'll know when the power's back.

If water lines could be impacted, you'll need to fill your tub and mood killer the line. Utilize this H2O for disinfection, similar to hand-washing and pouring down the restroom to flush it. If there's a possibility of flooding and you have the opportunity, move significant or difficult to-supplant things like workstations, collectibles, and treasures to upper floors to hold them back from getting water-logged.

Likewise, put resources into a reinforcement home generator to keep your home going through expanded blackouts.

6. PREP YOUR STORAGE ROOM.

If you are inside for some time, endure the hardship with supplement thick, rack stable things suggested by the Good Housekeeping Institute Nutrition Lab.

Food Shopping List:

- Canned fish/salmon
- Canned dark beans
- Olives
- Blended nuts
- Dry-cooked edamame
- Dry-cooked chickpeas
- Entire grain of recent rice
- Boxed grains like quinoa, buckwheat, or sorghum
- Olive oil
- Canola oil
- Low-salt veggie stock
- Canned tomatoes

- Canned veggies and other sound canned food sources
- Garlic powder
- Onion powder
- Stew preparing
- Salt
- Pepper
- Soy sauce
- Pureed tomatoes
- Ketchup
- Mustard

7. STORE EVERYTHING APPROPRIATELY.

How you store food can have an effect subsequently, as per the U.S. Branch of Agriculture Food Safety and Information Service (FSIS). If there's a possibility of flooding, make sure to store dry products in waterproof holders sufficiently high that they will be securely far removed from debased water.

Gathering food in the cooler can help it stay colder longer on account of a blackout. If you have preemptive guidance, freeze anything you don't need immediately, like extras, milk, and new meat and poultry, to keep them at a protected temperature longer. Stock your cooler with however much ice you can fit. Coolers loaded with ice can likewise be helpful if the power is out for over four hours.

Though you'll need to limit the sum you open and close your cooler entryway once the power goes out, FSIS suggests keeping a machine thermometer in your ice chest and cooler to help you decide whether food is protected. The cooler temperature should be lower than 40° Fahrenheit, and the cooler temperature should be below 0° Fahrenheit.

8. GET BACK SECURELY.

Returning home after a significant disaster can overwhelm you. Try not to allow your family to rush once again into your home without playing it safe.

Search for harm outside. Stroll around the outside and check for issues like free or fallen power links, harmed gas lines, and breaks in the establishment or in radiates. If you have trees close by, cautiously survey their dependability.

Note sounds and smells. If you smell gas or hear a murmuring commotion, call the local group of firefighters and have them drop by and review what is happening before you reemerge.

Then, take a look inside. If the power is still out, utilize an electric lamp (not a light — open blazes can consume things or influence gases to light) to evaluate the harm.

Examine apparatuses. For little machines like espresso producers and toaster ovens, take a gander at the lines for fraying or uncovered wires before utilizing them once more. Ice chests reach, and washers can be more convoluted; call a help organization to check the well-being of associations and parts, then supple whatever's seriously harmed.

Record the harm. It might be hard inwardly, yet if you need to document a protection guarantee, you'll require a visual record of all the harm with clear pictures and exhaustive notes before you tidy up.

HOW TO ORGANIZE YOUR HOME FOR WHEN IT IS NEEDED AND/OR HOW TO BUILD A FULLY EQUIPPED OFF-GRID (OFF-GRID) BUNKER

We comprehend that anticipating a horrendous event, such as a typhoon, is difficult for everybody; except toward the day's end, nothing remains but to plan for the most obviously terrible and anticipate the best.

Sorting out yourself and your family in anticipation of a natural disaster is significant.

1. STOCK UP ON A LOT OF FOOD

It means a lot to fill your cooler with whatever number of supplies could be expected under the circumstances. After a storm strikes, you don't have any idea how long you could do without power or how long it will require for supermarkets or service stations to open back up. Before the tempest, I went through my refrigerator and tossed out old food that might have possibly smelled up my ice chest if the power went out.

At that point, I accumulated all my canned food, durable food sources, water, sodas, and tidbits. I attempted to remain as solid as conceivable during the storm, so I made sure to have a lot of apples, avocados, bananas, and almonds.

2. GET INVENTIVE WHILE PUTTING AWAY WATER

Water bottles were particularly difficult for me to track down in stores, so rather than looking randomly for water bottles, I just topped off any suitable glass, tumbler, or pitcher in my kitchen cupboards and put them in the refrigerator.

3. GET GAS

I additionally attempted to keep away from the frenzy of the service stations. When the disaster was located, I promptly topped off my fuel tank. Likewise, there are choices accessible online to buy additional gas compartments and top them off as backup. I saw that specific individuals held on until the day of the tempest to get their gas, and by then, most service stations were out of assets. Remember that whoever wants it most will win in the end, so never look out for getting gas!

4. SET ASIDE ANYTHING INDIVIDUAL

I did a range of my home pre-typhoon with an end goal to keep away from inside harming my own things. I eliminated weak things, photo placements, and whatever was holding tight my dividers. At that point, I set these things away from compartments and kept them on the racks in my wardrobe.

5. LOAD UP ON LIGHT

We are mindful that blackouts for expanded timeframes are extremely normal during a storm, so I caught a lot of batteries, electric lamps, candles, matches, and lighters. I kept all my things in a cabinet to keep away from conceivable water harm.

6. REMAIN OCCUPIED

I also strived to keep myself and my family involved by planning indoor exercises during the tempest. Before the storm, I made sure to charge all my innovation gear, i.e., telephones, workstations, tablets, music gadgets, and DVD players. Tabletop games, books, and composing material were my redeeming quality when I was caught in my home without power.

7. SECURE EXCEEDINGLY SIGNIFICANT ARCHIVES AND INDIVIDUAL THINGS

Before the storm, I made a water-confirmation capacity canister for my significant records. This is an extraordinary method for getting yourself sorted and keeping your data in one secure location. I made different records for every one of my reports; for example,

- Banking Information
- Birth Certificates
- Visas
- Vehicle Information
- Protection, Water, and Electric Information

BUILDING THE BUNKER AND HOW TO ORGANIZE YOUR OFF-GRID AS BEST YOU CAN FOR THOSE WHO WILL HAVE TO LIVE IN IT

Bunkers are encountering a startling resurgence in the wake of becoming undesirable for a long time. Residents and government authorities fabricated various underground bunkers in the last 50% of the twentieth hundred years as fears of atomic conflict filled in the period after the Second World War. These designs, which range from simple substantial boxes to offices crossing tens of thousands of square feet, actually exist the whole way across the United States, though many have fallen into decay.

Many choose to have a project worker build underground bunkers, and there exists a whole industry around "extravagance bunkers," with Silicon Valley's wealthy people the primary clients. These offices in far-off locations are loaded with conveniences and cost a few million bucks.

With a touch of readiness, a sensible financial plan, and some difficult work, nonetheless, building your own underground bunker on your own property is conceivable. You needn't bother with planning for the apocalypse to have a valid justification for building a bunker, as these designs have horde utilizes. Bunkers can offer security from various cataclysmic events like typhoons and cyclones, also as control fires and quakes, which can leave different sorts of designs unsound in the prompt repercussions.

While choosing to build your own bunker, the accompanying steps are fundamental:

1. GET PERMISSION

The main thing to do is to get the appropriate licenses. Grants are utilized to guarantee security for yourself and everybody around you during the undertaking. Inability to get or conform to a grant can be costly and, at times, hazardous if you're not cautious.

Instead, you would not begin digging and building an underground bunker just to be halted and compelled to pay a mighty fine. Now and again, you'll be compelled to eliminate or fix any venture you set off on a mission to do.

To acquire the fitting licenses, you need to go to your neighborhood building division or building official. You should show them plans of what you will be doing, so make sure you have your outline (favoring that later) and a guide showing where you will work.

Grants can change contingent upon where you reside; for instance, if you're building your bunker in San Diego, CA, the sorts of licenses you'll require are:

REVIEWING PERMIT: Grading is required when a task might modify the geology of a property because of unearthing or fillings. A starter assessment is expected to ensure you're not building on earth's delicate terrains and survey the possibility of the task you're leading.

BUILDING PERMIT: This guarantees that the development project agrees with nearby, state, and government regulations.

OPTIONAL PERMIT: An optional grant is required when a task has the chance to influence the encompassing region because of the proposed use, location, or configuration highlight.

PLUMBING PERMIT: A pipe grant is fundamental if you're adding plumbing to your underground bunker (erring on that later).

ELECTRICAL PERMIT: If you introduce any electrical wiring or hardware, you'll require an electrical grant to make sure everything is wired securely and accurately.

Regardless of where you're found, you really have to call 811 before you dig, so you don't unintentionally break an underground utility line. Doing so can be outrageous and risky to your well-being. It'll require a couple of days, yet a finder can identify the position of any underground utility.

---

2. PICK THE LOCATION

When you have your licenses set up, the next thing you have to do is to think about your bunker location. It should be somewhere you'll be protected and private if the mystery is a fundamental component.

Keep away from any spot that is near enormous waterways as they're bound to flood, which can harm the underlying honesty of your bunker. In like manner, keep away from any combustible spot.

Don't dive into a spot that is encircled by trees and vegetation. Digging close to trees implies that you'll manage a convoluted snare of roots that will be difficult to slice through. That and slicing through these roots can be unfavorable to the neighborhood geology.

Moreover, you have to try not to dive into any utility lines. If you called 811, you'd definitely know precisely where the utilities are found. Try not to dig on top or with 18-24″ on all sides of the utility line. If you can't stay away from them, you might have to reevaluate where you build your bunker.

3. FOSTER A BLUEPRINT

Very much like while you're building a house, you initially ought to foster a diagram of your underground bunker. In any case, not at all like a house; you're not building for extravagance, yet instead for wellbeing and security.

Pick where you will build your bunker, away from waterways, power lines, and trees. From that point, you'll get a feeling of how you can plan your outline.

There won't be much room; however, that doesn't mean you can't make it work. You need to have adequate space to not embrace your knees all over; however, you would rather not waste space.

Consider it a little house and utilize similar tips to boost space. For instance:

- Consolidate spaces by utilizing an open region plan
- Use vertical space for capacity proficiency.
- Introduce divider-mounted furniture like a work area or table to save money on space.

Anything you choose to do, make sure you plan for both productivity and solace. You might be building a bunker for wellbeing; however, that doesn't mean you need to make it feel claustrophobic.

To keep away from claustrophobia, however much as could be expected while using the restricted measure of room you have, FEMA suggests between 5-10 square feet for each individual for twister or typhoon shelters. Considering this, attempt to make arrangements for that much confidential space per individual.

4. PICK THE RIGHT BUNKER BUILDING MATERIAL

Make sure the bunker is made of significant areas of strength that will not disintegrate under the soil. Not all building materials are equivalent, particularly with regards to managing building something underground. The most well-known building materials are:

METAL SHEETING: Metal sheeting is durable and water-safe; however, it can likewise be costly, particularly since protection should be added.

BLOCKS: Bricks are strong and moderately suitable building materials that are extraordinary separators and unimaginably weatherproof. They can likewise add style and variety to a generally grim circumstance.

CONCRETE: Reinforced cement can endure high loads and is somewhat modest. Self-mending concrete is a high-level building material that lessens support prerequisites and has around a 200-year lifespan.

Try not to utilize wood, as it's amazingly inclined to endure decay and can become helpless against invasion. You can utilize wood to enliven your bunker, yet make sure you keep it clean.

Transporting compartment bunkers can be roomy and financially savvy. Notwithstanding, you won't have the option to modify your format. Delivering compartments would likewise be supported as delivery holders aren't worked to be covered.

Now all that remains is to move on to the next step. Find a way to dig into the ground.

5. PICK THE RIGHT EXCAVATING EQUIPMENT

Unless you have absolutely no worries to speak of, a digging tool isn't adequate enough for the job needing to be done. You want exhuming gear that can both dig rapidly and in abnormal or restricted spaces. Since you're holding back nothing speed of work while you're digging, you will need a digger and an earthmover.

There are five principal uses of a digger: cutting asphalt, making waste, scooping, digging for utility lines, and cutting roots. While digging for your bunker, a digger can help by framing the region where you need to put your bunker.

Backhoes are flexible earthmoving machines utilized for anything from digging a channel to mining tasks. Because there are different sorts of backhoes accessible, you'll have the option to utilize one to really recover an opening for your bunker.

You'll begin by estimating and setting up an edge for the dig. Then utilize the digger to frame. From that point onward, you can utilize an earthmover to start uncovering the remainder of the opening your bunker will be set.

A backhoe will give a substantially more effective and precise dig because of its natural movement of digging. A scaled-down backhoe can fit in tight spaces and are more qualified for digging openings in off-kilter regions, like a terrace.

6. GAIN KEY LIVING MATERIALS

Placing a metal box on the ground and throwing in the towel isn't sufficient. An underground bunker needs to support you and your friends and family for a significant time frame. The five things you need to make sure that you incorporate are:

VENTILATION AND AIR FILTERS: These channels ventilate clean air into your bunker. An N.B.C. (Natural, Biological, Chemical) channel is your smartest choice to safeguard your shelter from air impurities and give natural air.

GENERATOR: This will give power to your bunker. To decide how much power you will require, including the total wattage of all that utilizes power.

This will provide you with a comprehension of how to pick the best generator for your bunker. Consider introducing a solar generator to try not to reserve fuel or keep it around as a reinforcement.

WATER FILTERS: These will keep a solid wellspring of clean water close by. Any water channel can work, yet a UV channel is ideal for an underground bunker. They utilize different frequencies of UV light to free the water of infections and microorganisms.

WASTE REMOVAL SYSTEM: Mismanaging waste can be negative to one's well-being. For an underground bunker, there are a couple of choices you can go with:

You can keep it basic with a room with a channel, similar to a restroom. It's modest and speedy; however, it tends to be unsanitary.

A "crap tube" is a speedy method for managing waste, and they're not difficult to make, requiring just some PVC pipe. They're not perfect for long-term use, nonetheless.

A treating the soil latrine needs no water; all things considered, it changes waste into manure, which is brilliant if you have plants, yet they can be a little expensive and foul in encased places.

A wastewater siphon and lift framework is a well-known choice for controlling waste. These frameworks siphon waste from lower to higher rises.

Likewise, you'll need to load up on filtered water and individual and durable food. Try not to keep a tight budget on any of these; they will safeguard your shelter and every one of the occupants.

7. BEGIN DIGGING

When you, at long last, start to dig, you'll use the cut and cover strategy (like how trams are assembled). In this technique, you dig a channel, make an emotionally supportive network (favoring that later), place your bunker and cover it back up.

However, before you kick things off, we should rapidly survey the digging security. As per OSHA, digging is one of the riskiest development occupations, so make sure you're working on digging well-being by introducing defensive frameworks to prevent collapses. The three most normal defensive frameworks are inclining/sidelining, shoring, and introducing a channel safeguard.

Slanting includes cutting the channel divider at a point to make a slant, whereas sidelining is the demonstration of making long seats/steps to go up the divider.

Shoring is the demonstration of building an emotionally supportive network to keep the soil set up, preventing a breakdown.

A channel safeguard, or channel box, shields the individual inside from a collapse instead of being used to prevent one. Utilize this related to the next two defensive frameworks.

Remember to consider how deep your bunker will be. You need to dig adequately profound to safeguard yourself from indigenous habitats; however, not excessively profound with the goal that you risk catching yourself.

A basic guideline of thumb is that the highest point of your bunker ought to have something like 10 feet of stuffed soil on top. Dry, pressed soil is hotter than free soil and can safeguard against radiation and impact waves. If you really need to recover yourself for reasons unknown, you will not have a ton of soil on top of you.

8. SUPPORT THE SHELTER

Supporting your shelter is a vital step in building an underground bunker. Regardless of how profound you dig, you will have a lot of weight pushing down from the top because of soil, water, vegetation, and other external items.

Start by setting up a legitimate establishment before setting up your shelter to help your bunker. Concrete is probably the best material for an entire establishment, yet it can be inclined to break. Utilize built-up concrete or self-mending concrete for more prominent outcomes.

Place metal shafts across the channel to help your bunker against imploding. You can likewise utilize supported cement to make an additional external layer for added security.

The dividers of your bunker should additionally be somewhere around 1-3 feet thick. If you're utilizing metal sheets, add a layer of block or substantial inside. If you're utilizing concrete, make sure that the dividers are thick and built up to add additional insurance against dangerous shockwaves and radiation.

Water harm can make form if untreated and obliterate your designs. Cover your bunker and defensive frameworks with waterproof materials, like rubber, treated black-top, or cementitious waterproof covering.

If you're building in a seismic tremor inclined region, consider using comparable supported techniques as resistant to quake buildings. Shear dividers, cross supports, and second opposing casings can rearrange the seismic powers, safeguarding the bunker.

Whether it's thermal radiation or a prophetically catastrophic situation, you will invest some energy underneath your bunker during the underlying event. At the absolute minimum, FEMA suggests you ought to have something like fourteen days of food and water per individual.

Regardless of the situation, you ought to apply the 7:10 guideline utilized to appraise radioactive gamble. It expresses that for each 7-overlay expansion in time after the explosion, there is a 10-crease expansion in the explosion.

Fundamentally, if two hours have passed after the explosion, the radiation openness rate is 400 roentgens (radioactive waves) each hour. Following 14 hours, the radioactive openness rate is 1/10 of that.

Make sure the food is sound and will endure, nonetheless. A rundown of the best, durable food varieties include:

- Dried/canned beans
- Dried/canned foods grown from the ground
- Dried/canned meats
- Peanut butter
- Nuts/seeds
- Grains
- Protein bars
- Canned soup
- Non-dairy and dry milk

Ensure you're regularly restocking and supplanting your food varieties; you would rather not eat any spoiled food when a crisis occurs.

You ought to likewise keep a microwave or other crisis cooking arrangements like canned heat or a convenient butane oven. Candles can likewise be utilized as a type of slow cooking and are a dependable wellspring of light if the power goes out. Put a can or pot on an oven mesh and spot the light underneath.

The water is particularly significant as radiation can keep on pouring down for around 24 hours after an explosion. You ought to likewise think about loading up on nutrients and different enhancements.

Similarly, your underground shelter doesn't need to be a cold and bleak spot. You should give your best to prevent any mental harm from disconnection. Restlessness is a well-known term that refers to the pessimistic sensations of separation. It can cause:

- Fretfulness
- Peevishness
- Difficulty concentrating
- Dormancy
- Sorrow

Hang up pictures, introduce a speaker framework to play music, or add an exercise region to keep yourself occupied. Your emotional well-being is just about as significant as your actual well-being, so make sure you deal with your psychological prosperity.

The COVID-19 pandemic has caused much stress over their security and prosperity. Figuring out how to build an underground bunker can set you up for any crisis. All you want now is the right gear and a strategy.

BOOK 3: RV AND OFF-GRID SHELTERS

HOW TO TURN ANY RIG AND RV INTO A FULLY EQUIPPED OFF-GRID SHELTER

An RV is one of the least demanding and most daring lifestyle choices. Whether it's a 6-month journey the nation over or a three-road trip to a nearby state park, RVs have all you really need to mix indoor and open-air life. They're lodges on wheels, with beds, showers, restrooms, and almost full kitchens. Many RV clients still intensely depend on associations and hookups to give power and water.

What happens when you need to branch out of the universe of full campsites and into the universe of public land? An irregular field in Montana won't have a spot to plug into or a direct hose line with new water.

Solar energy is the essential extra you really want for an off-framework lifestyle; however, it's, by all accounts, not the only interesting point.

WHAT IS AN RV?

RV represents a racing vehicle. An RV is a wheeled unit with living quarters utilized for sporting purposes like setting up camp and voyaging. A few RVs have incorporated drive frameworks, while others require vans, trucks, or SUVs to pull them around.

Grid's meaning could be a little clearer.

Living off-matrix implies you are not utilizing the public lattice of utilities, specifically power. Off-network implies no direct water line, no power, and no garbage removal. In the RV world, this is some of the time likewise referred to as boondocking, free setting up camp or dry setting up camp.

A fifth-wheel RV is stopped among prickly plants in the desert.

While setting up camp anyplace, consistently follow the "leave no follow" rules.

WHAT IS REQUIRED FOR OFF-GRID RV LIVING?

To carry on with life as regularly as conceivable while off-framework adventuring, you really need to track down answers for the shortfall of fitting and-play utility associations. As such, your RV needs its own wellspring of power, its own wellspring of water, and its own strategy for dealing with waste.

NEW WATER STORAGE TANK

This isn't old America where you could just put a reed straw into a stream and drink or plunge into a lake and scrub down. You really need to convey your spotless water with you inside the RV. You'll involve it for cooking, for drinking, for the restroom, for the shower, and for whatever else new water is required. RVs have water capacity frameworks included; however additional items never hurt anyone.

WASTE STORAGE TANKS

Your RV has a restroom; it simply doesn't have a line that stretches out from that latrine to a waste management office. Your waste goes into a capacity box that is subsequently discharged at a dump site. If you're going off-lattice, you need to understand how much waste your RV can store and that you are so near the closest dump site.

POWER

Unless you're going into the wild, you'll, in any case, need and use power while you're enjoying the great outdoors. You could require it for lights, a fridge, warming, charging telephones, or different reasons. Your best two choices for obtaining power without a fitting are fuel or potentially the sun.

GAS GENERATOR

Using a gas generator is a more seasoned technique that is more required than utilizing solar power. Generators are huge, weighty, noisy, and require gas tops off, so they're not great for voyaging, manageability, or keeping up with the feeling of harmony and calm such countless individuals want from nature.

SOLAR

Depending on sun accessibility, solar power is possibly the best technique for controlling your off-framework RV. Solar age utilizes boards to catch daylight and convert it into energy, which is then put away in a battery pack. Contingent on the number of apparatuses you have and use and the everyday luxuries you expect for day-to-day existence, you can utilize convenient solar units or frameworks incorporated into the RV.

KINDS OF SOLAR SYSTEMS

There are a couple of choices when picking how to use solar in an RV. Some are modest and straightforward; others are more costly and involved. Realize which is best for you.

COMPACT AFTERMARKET

If you don't need a lot of energy, you could pull off utilizing a compact solar pack. These gadgets commonly highlight a couple of solar boards that can be collapsed or pressed into a stowable unit.

Masters: Simple arrangement, modest, saves space, adaptable, not devoted to RV, can follow daylight, more straightforward to spotless, ready to point toward sun, direct attachments.

Cons: insufficient power for apparatuses, additional arrangement work.

COORDINATED AFTERMARKET

If you require the greatest measure of conceivable energy, you will need an expertly introduced solar framework that coordinates with your RV electrical framework. The fundamental parts will be the solar boards, the charging unit, the battery pack, and an inverter. The boards regularly go on the top of the RV, while the spare parts live inside the vehicle.

Aces: You can get the precisely exact thing you want, you can pick where to store the gear, and you pick the brands and providers

Cons: Expensive, more muddled, managing reseller's exchange shops.

MANUFACTURING PLANT INTEGRATED

Certain makers, for example, the Keystone RV Company, offer solar frameworks directly from the plant. This is an incredible choice because everything is set up and incorporated into your RV; however, it probably won't have the specific gear you need. Thus, getting a good course and purchasing directly from the factory may be more costly. These could likewise be more difficult to overhaul from here on out, as solar power is steadily becoming more proficient and less expensive.

Experts: No bothering with reseller's exchange shops; totally coordinated, custom-fitted for your RV

Cons: Possibly more costly, zero power over the arrangement, potentially difficult to change.

HOW MANY SOLAR PANELS ARE NEEDED?

Basic solar units utilize one solar board, while cutting-edge frameworks top off the whole rooftop with panels. An unpleasant normal is 1-4 boards, regularly evaluated around 100 watts each. The number of solar boards you require for your experience will rely upon your battery limit, what machines you intend to utilize, the amount you depend on common luxuries, and where long you'll be going off-network.

This RV solar adding machine from GoPower requests that various prompts decide what you really want.

What is the cost of an RV Solar System?

Hope to pay between $500-$2,500 for each of the pieces of a solar framework, excluding the work of the establishment.

WARNS FOR MAXIMIZING AND PRESERVING ENERGY GRID

The following are a couple of quick ways to help you keep up with the energy your solar framework made.

- Camp in unbiased environments
- Driven lighting
- No AC or warming
- High-effectiveness machines
- Do things physically without power whenever the situation allows
- Possibly charge gadgets when not being used
- Point and move compact boards with the sun over the day.

THINGS TO CHECK BEFORE BUYING AN RV

Is the street requiring experience? If you say yes, then an RV may be an incredible choice for your off-framework setting up camp. It is, in any case, fundamental to recall that purchasing an RV can be trying with countless such models that are accessible on the lookout.

It is once in a while moderately difficult to perceive whether the nature of a specific RV is sufficient to purchase in a solitary look. So before making a venture, here are the elements that you ought to really investigate if you are buying an RV.

1. HOW MIGHT YOU USE IT?

In purchasing an RV, you ought to ask yourself whether you will utilize it only for setting up camp or for off-lattice living. Typically, a setting up camp experience can keep going for about fourteen days. It is also fundamental to consider the number of basics you bring and the individuals you are going with. This is an amazing method for figuring out what size of RV is great for your associates and your spending plan.

2. CHECK FOR MAINTENANCE RECORDS

Support records are beyond a shadow of a doubt, the main thing that you ought to take a gander at before purchasing an RV. An organization or somebody happy with the usefulness of their RV will elect to show you the support records of the vehicle. By looking at an RV's support records, you can guarantee that the vehicle won't create any issues if you choose to have off-matrix setting up camp with your loved ones.

While analyzing the records, consistently search for the steadiness in oil changes with the goal that you can completely perceive if they were changed routinely and as per the maker's recommendation. As well as checking the recurrence of oil transforms, it is likewise critical to see whether the crankshaft belt has been modified, mainly if the vehicle is right within or over 60,000 miles.

3. CAUTIOUSLY CHECK FOR LEAKS AND ODORS

This is particularly prudent if you are buying a pre-owned RV. Continuously make sure that each part of the vehicle is all together and has no issues that could demolish your off-lattice setting up camp. I strongly suggest that you examine the scents, molds, breaks, canopies, and the top of the RV before going with a buy choice.

It would be helpful if you carried somebody with you to ensure that nothing was missed during the examination. Furthermore, bring electric lamps that will help you look at the apparatus and the dim spots of the RV.

If your spending plan is tight, choosing RVs with a couple of issues can be helpful on your part (contingent upon the expense of fixes, obviously). Would it be advisable for you to feel that there are many such issues and the cost is exceptionally high? It is ideal for haggling with the dealer to make sure that you set aside cash simultaneously.

4. ASSESS THE TIRES

Searching for mileage on tires is basic, particularly if you need to buy a recycled RV. No matter what the quality and the wear of the tire, it is ideal for the proprietor to supplant the tire once like clockwork. Tires are very costly if you are driving top-class apparatuses, and replacing them could cost you dearly.

One of the fastest ways of inspecting the nature of the tire is to utilize your hands to detect cracks or blames. Aside from examining the vehicle's tires, it is also best to review the extra tire to guarantee that all tires have similar makes and models.

One more simple method for deciding the greatness of a tire is by determining its age. You can undoubtedly know the tire's age by essentially taking a gander at letters and numbers imbued on their sidewalls. Generally speaking, a tire has "US DOT" alongside a four-digit number which demonstrates the date it was fabricated.

5. REQUEST A TEST DRIVE

You have investigated every one of the parts, and everything appears to look at your rundown. Now, one thing should be finished, and that is asking the dealer for a test drive. A test drive will permit you to get the vibe of the RV out and about and your capacity to drive it effortlessly and accurately. This can be the game changer whether full-time RV living is for you.

Drive the RV on open streets (particularly if you are driving it interestingly) to perceive how it can deal with different rates and slow down and turn. The best way to painstakingly tune in for things is by bobbing or shaking when the RV moves. It is important to note that the RV you will test is likely to be lightweight. You must consider that the RV will weigh considerably more once you load all your belongings into it.

Typically, you don't need to purchase an RV immediately. Perhaps you need to test whether an RV life is excellent for you. Maybe you need to check a specific RV model before buying it. In such cases, go to RVshare and pick an RV to lease. This site has a remarkable decision of sporting vehicles you lease straightforwardly from proprietors close to you.

RV FEATURES THAT REALLY MATTER

In picking an RV, usefulness and the home inclination it emits are among the things that ought to be considered seriously. Here are highlights that each RV ought to have.

1. WATER TANKS

Water tanks typically change as per the size of an RV. It is, in every case, very critical to go for an RV with water tanks that can undoubtedly be associated with outside water frameworks. Along these lines, you can get a new and steady water supply, mainly if you are living in off-framework trailers.

Cleaning and utilizing sanitizers on water tanks are maybe the main part of your RV water framework upkeep. Continuously ensure that waste water or dark water is appropriated in pipes that are inverse to your drinking water to avoid sicknesses and destructive illnesses.

I would suggest getting an A.A 16 Gallon RV Fresh/Gray Water Tank for your RV (on Amazon). It's a 16-gallon dependable tank produced using solid polyethylene, supported by the FDA. This tank is developed as one piece, so you don't need to stress that it might burst at creases - there are essentially no creases. The tank can be effectively introduced and opposes erosion, rust, and stains. A phenomenal decision for your manufactured home!

2. RESTROOM

Having a restroom is probably the most significant advantage of RV travel. A greater part of off-matrix trailers accompanies a proper washroom with a restroom you can shower and sit on. At the same time, they don't take much space; more modest RV restrooms are ordinarily confined to a bit of space, and all that in the room will get wet.

If you need great measured restrooms, it is constantly prescribed to pursue huge RVs since it has a little bath or stand-up shower, an additional restroom, and a sink.

Concerning washing your garments, maybe a decent versatile washing machine will end up being sufficient.

3. POWER

Quite a long time ago, a commonplace camper didn't have power. I question that such an arrangement can work for everybody nowadays. The majority of the RVs now have some power source. For example, a major DC battery. Numerous campgrounds provide you with AC power through hookups, so RV makers added AC/DC converters, and now you can charge your battery and have a lovely stay inside.

However, if your RV is furnished with a wide range of machines, a 12-volt battery probably won't be sufficient. A ton of RVs accompanies an inherent generator. It permits individuals to travel a lot further and be free of electrical hookups. It runs your cooler, TV, PC, and even your toaster oven and espresso maker. It's your power plant!

Notice that a generator requires fuel, typically propane, diesel, or gas. Along these lines, you should top off your fuel holders every once.

Likewise, you ought to consider getting a compact solar board to help your power framework.

4. SLIDE OUTS

One of the most alluring highlights of an RV is slide-outs. Conventionally, a slide-out can help extend the size of an RV and make it appear to be bigger than it truly is. It is, nonetheless, vital to remember that slides will decisively build the heaviness of your apparatus, so it is smarter to stop in a spot with an adequate measure of room to slide them out.

Utilizing a slide-out will continually require ordinary upkeep. To drag out its condition, it is recommended to use a conditioner two times every year to wash its seals.

5. KITCHEN

Rough terrain trailers likewise have kitchens that are ordinarily included a refrigerator, a decent sink, and a wide scope of cooking machines. An extraordinary RV kitchen will again include a cupboard where you can put your dishes, cutting sheets, cups, Tupperware compartments, espresso pots, and skillet, among others.

As a rule, coolers found in current RV frameworks are worked through power and gas. Likewise, you can decide to introduce a little generator in your kitchen if you choose to add a microwave.

6. RV SECURITY

Your RV should be gotten around evening time, or when you pass on it to climb by walking. Never leave your assets and your friends and family unprotected. There is a profoundly evaluated item on Amazon, RVLock Key Fob, and RH Compact Keyless Entry Keypad. It fits practically any sporting vehicle and guards your entrance door. You can introduce it in minutes and have a solid sense of reassurance until the end of your excursion. Incorporates a keyless handle, a keypad with north of 1 million potential codes, a remote coxcomb (amount to 10), mechanical keys, and 4 AA batteries. An ideal arrangement that deals with your RV wellbeing and security consistently.

7. CELLAR STORAGE

Another element a great RV has is a pleasant storm cellar capacity where you can keep your seats, floor coverings, open-air tables, cogwheels, and bikes. Class A RVs have a greater cellar and a lot bigger extra room than different kinds of rough terrain trailers. There are some class C RVs that have a sizable measure of room for your different utilities.

8. FLOORING

The ground surface of an RV ought to be adaptable in view of your likings and preferences. This is a compelling method for modernizing your RV with a choice of a recently redesigned look. Customarily, eliminating and supplanting the ground surface plan of your floor covering can be finished without help from anyone else in under no time.

9. RESTING AREA

This simply should be obvious. Your home on wheels should have a bed. When we consider home or even search for lodging, the bed is the focal piece that transforms any four dividers into a spot reasonable for individuals.

Normally, simply a bed isn't sufficient unless you're on a limited financial plan. It's particularly obvious if there should be an occurrence of a family. What you truly need is a room, a space separate from different spaces within the RV. Family RVs frequently have at least two rooms for guardians as well with respect to youngsters.

I would propose that you likewise ensure you're getting an RV with a stroll around the bed. Unless you need to save money on space and get an especially little RV, this is an unquestionable requirement. If it's a bed for two, then every accomplice will get their own bed approach without the need for jumping over the other's space. This additionally makes the task of bed-making a lot simpler.

Lastly, if you need security for the little ones, your room should be placed through an entryway and not a shade. Some RV vendors supplant the entryways with shades to make the vehicle lighter. I don't believe that you ought to think twice about your security.

10. SEATING AND DINING AREA

This is another significant RV game plan that totally relies on the number of individuals that will travel together. Moreover, you could have visitors now and then. Each relative and guest ought to have their own seat for eating and unwinding. Consider these variables and afterward settle on the size, amount, and plan of the seating places. If you introduce a TV or a computer game control center, see whether the seats face the diversion community appropriately.

THE MOST EFFECTIVE METHOD TO START LIVING IN AN OFF-GRID RV

1. SCOUT THE LOCATION

Your most memorable choice ought to be the area. The excellence of an RV is that you have the opportunity of versatility. You can continuously find a parking space or a camping area where you go through an evening or two and afterward drive on to another objective. There are public grounds across the USA where you can reside and park free of charge, although I do accept that they are restricted to a 14-day stay. I examined free parking spots in an article about an independent RV. Likewise, there is the choice of buying your property, where your vehicle can be left endlessly.

After you choose where you will stop, research the climate of the close-by area. What's it like there in the evenings? Cold, hot, or sticky evenings can adversely influence resting outside in an RV. Then, at that point, current RVs accompany extraordinary divider confinement, cooling, warmers, etc. In any case, conclude whether the neighborhood environment will suit your preferences. Not every person enjoys and endures each conceivable climate.

Track down the area of significant-close by offices. You would have to find every vital structure, like a market and a clinical office. Moreover, if you would instead not burn through 24 hours in the RV and need a break from investigating nature, see what diversion is presented by the ongoing region: film and regular theaters, cafés, event congregations, etc.

2. SET UP YOUR RV

As you plan to live off the lattice, look hard and long at your RV and choose what devices and gear it needs before heading for the street. Utensils, plates, fixing instruments, electric machines, etc. Do you have a rug? Then you ought to get a vacuum cleaner. Wood flooring? Pack a brush. Make an intensive shopping list, and don't leave for the street until you've crossed out every one of the things.

Also, look at your RV's offices. Should the water tank be renewed with new water? Perhaps it needs some chlorine for extra purification. Was the sewer tank discharged? If not, visit an unloading station as you drive out. Check the propane tanks and fill them, if essential. Undoubtedly re-energize all RV batteries.

After this is all finished, you are all set.

3. SETTLE AND ESTABLISH ROUTINES

Test different ways of stopping whenever you've shown up to your chosen area, so you utilize the light and the shade of this spot entirely. If it's your highly durable property, think about making a cushion for the RV to remain on. If there are individuals living close by, check whether you can make a few new companions, they can have a ton of valuable data about this area.

Lay out schedules that will keep your RV and its offices in top shape. Consistently look at oil, tires, gas, and so forth as you do with a normal vehicle. Make a timetable and focus on it: routinely void the sewer, top off water and propane, and purchase food.

If you plan to leave sooner or later, ensure you leave the region flawless clean. We need no adverse consequences on the climate. Rehash stages 1 and 2 and be headed to opportunity.

Might You at any point Fully Live Off the Grid in an RV?

This is an inquiry that merits a unique consideration. How about we believe that you've picked the right RV, got all of the vital instruments and hardware, and are now out and about. You stop at whatever point you can and live a lease-free, power matrix-free life. Yet, might you at any moment be 100 percent off the lattice?

The short response is that it is conceivable with a great, current RV. Notwithstanding, there are a few additional means that you need to take.

RV CAMPING TERMINOLOGY

For RV setting up camp, a few terms you will need to know are:

BACK-IN SITE: When looking for an RV camping area, you might hear some destinations portrayed as back-in locales. These campgrounds require the RV driver to uphold them. RV camping areas can likewise be "get through destinations," which the driver can enter from one end and exit from the other.

BOONDOCKING: Also called "dry setting up camp," boondocking portrays RV setting up camp in camping areas with no electric, water, or sewer hookups. Boondocking permits RVers to camp in distant regions by depending on the independent offices in their RV.

FULL HOOKUP: RV camping areas depicted as full hookup locales will approach the campsite's electric, water and sewer supplies. RVers setting up camp at full hookup locales will need to associate with these utilities for simplicity and are open to setting up camp.

HULA SKIRT: RVs can kick up a ton of trash and stones when going on rough or dusty streets. A hula skirt can be connected to the back guard of an RV to prevent this garbage from hitting vehicles behind any trailer.

RIG: Rig is one of the many setting up camp terms used to refer to an RV. Whether you call your RV an apparatus, trailer, camper, or RV, anything that RV epithet you pick ultimately depends on you and your setting up camp style.

INDEPENDENT: While most RVs utilize outside hookups to get to utilities at a campsite, a few RVs can supply their electric, waste, and water needs. These RVs are called independent RVs and can be an extraordinary choice for those more open to boondocking.

SLIDE-OUT: Some special RVs have slide-outs that can be pushed on a mission to extend the accessible living space and afterward withdrawn while voyaging.

SNOWBIRD: Snowbird refers to a term used to depict RVers who travel south in the colder time of year to get away from the colder climate up north.

TOY HAULER: An RV that is equipped for conveying cruisers, soil bicycles, ATVs, or other external "toys" within it is in many cases called a toy hauler. These RVs have a huge inside space intended for safely moving hardware for individuals who love the external experience.

UNDERSIDE: The floor surface or underside of an RV is, in many cases, called the bottom. The RV underside incorporates water hoses, pipes, and different valves. In the colder time of year, RVers who desire to continue to utilize their RV frequently add defensive material to the RV underside.

WINTERIZING: Those who need to utilize their RV lasting through the year might have to add a few insurances from the snow and climate and set up their RV for the virus. Those putting away their RV for the colder season ought to likewise go to lengths to guarantee their camper is safeguarded in the colder time of year. This course of setting up an RV for winter is, in many cases, called winterizing. If you have any desire to skip winterizing your RV, become a snowbird and go to a hotter climate.

BOOK 4: MANAGING YOUR SHELTER'S WATER SUPPLY

Water is our most significant asset, yet no one can tell when a debacle could think twice about neighborhood water supply. While the novel Covid has not been recognized in drinking water supplies, as per the World Health Organization, many of you have connected about emergency water sift choices as you work through your fiasco packs. I've put together the data you want on some clean water answers to help guarantee you approach water safe to drink during a wide range of crises.

CLEAN WATER THREATS

While drinking water is contaminated in civil or created regions, the immediate danger to human wellbeing is the presentation of waterborne microbes — tiny sickness-causing bugs. These incorporate microorganisms, protozoa, and infections, which are all ordinarily eliminated by the city treatment focus well before water at any point streams out of your tap.

In a catastrophe circumstance, pollution of the current metropolitan water supply can happen rapidly. For instance, a sewer line can break, intermixing sewage with your clean water supply and presenting those pathogenic specialists.

Cataclysmic events can harm the scope of water frameworks. If, for instance, a tremor or avalanche sends garbage or residue into a repository or breaks a water fundamental, you could be compelled to source drinking water from surface water, which is unsafe to drink without treatment.

In filthy circumstances — particularly following cataclysmic events — unfortunate disinfection can rapidly prompt human and creature waste to blend in with the drinking water. Being ready for the surprising will help guarantee that you and your family stay away from ailment from the water you drink.

GETTING READY FOR A WATER EMERGENCY

A singular's water needs will differ depending on age, well-being, and environment (water requirements can be twofold in hot temperatures). Yet, as a rule, you ought to make arrangements for at least one gallon of water for every individual each day to be utilized for drinking and disinfection purposes (food prep, washing dishes, cleaning teeth, etc.). The best arrangement is to stock a stockpile of store-purchased water (with termination dates clearly set apart) in a cool, dull spot. The CDC suggests having a three-day supply close by essentially.

But since you don't have the foggiest idea how long you could be without water, having a water treatment arrangement, an individual, convenient treatment framework that will eliminate waterborne microbes and other potential contaminants is likewise significant. These include

- Infections (for example, norovirus, rotavirus, and hepatitis A) spread to people by human waste
- Microbes (for example, Salmonella and E. coli): Spread by people and creatures
- Protozoa (for example, Giardia and Cryptosporidium) spread by people and creatures
- Residue/soil/sediment: Not especially hurtful to wellbeing, yet unsavory or hindering
- Organics (for example, oil, herbicides, pesticides, weighty metals, and different synthetic substances) harmful with rehashed openness

Your emergency water treatment arrangement should make preparations for the initial three (the bugs) to shield you from a quick ailment, yet it's ideal for eliminating everything if you would be able. There are different choices for arriving.

The most effective method to MANAGE YOUR SHELTER'S WATER SUPPLY

If you are in a catastrophe or emergency, you should do whatever it may take to prevent the disease from unsafe water.

After a fiasco

Try not to utilize water you suspect or have been told is contaminated to drink, wash dishes, clean your teeth, wash and plan food, clean up, make ice, or make child equations.

Utilize bottled, boiled, or treated water for drinking, cooking, and individual cleanliness.

Follow your state, neighborhood, or ancestral wellbeing division for specific proposals in regards to bubbling or treating water in your space.

Try not to drink liquor. Liquor gets dried out of the body, which builds the requirement for drinking water.

During a water-related emergency or episode, clean drinking water may not be accessible. Set yourself up for an emergency by making and putting away a stockpile of water that will address your family's issues.

Bottled Water

Unopened economically, bottled water is the safest and most dependable wellspring of water in an emergency. If you don't have bottled water, you can make your water safe to drink by adhering to the guidelines recorded on our Making Water Safe in an Emergency page and utilizing clean containers to gather and store your water.

THE AMOUNT OF EMERGENCY WATER TO STORE

- Store something like 1 gallon of water for every individual for three days, mainly for drinking and sterilization.
- Attempt to store a 2-week supply if conceivable.

- Think about putting away more water than this for sweltering environments, pregnant ladies, and people who are wiped out.
- Notice the termination date for store-purchased water.
- Supplant non-store-purchased water like clockwork.
- Store a jug of unscented fluid family chlorine dye (mark ought to say it contains somewhere in the range of 5% and 9% of sodium hypochlorite) to sanitize your water, if vital, and to use for general cleaning and disinfecting.

PICKING A CONTAINER

While putting away safe water (water that has been blessed to make it safe to utilize), it is ideal to use food-grade water storage containers, which don't move harmful substances into the water they are holding. FDA-supported food-grade storage containers can be found in excess or set up a camp stockpile stores. Contact the maker if you don't know if a storage holder is food grade. If you can't utilize a food-grade water storage holder, be sure the compartment you pick:

- Has a top that can be shut firmly
- It is made of solid, rugged materials (i.e., not glass)
- If conceivable, utilize a holder with a restricted neck or opening so water can be spilled out.
- Try not to USE containers utilized to hold fluid or strong poisonous synthetic compounds (dye, pesticides, etc.)

CLEANING AND SANITIZING A WATER STORAGE CONTAINER BEFORE USE

Before loading up with safe water, utilize these means to clean and disinfect water storage containers:

Wash the storage holder and flush it totally with water.

Disinfect the holder with an answer made by blending one teaspoon of unscented fluid family chlorine bleach in 1 quart of water. Use dye that contains 5%-9% sodium hypochlorite.

Cover the compartment firmly and shake it well. Ensure the cleaning bleach arrangement contacts generally inside surfaces of the compartment.

Stand by around 30 seconds, and afterward, spill the disinfecting arrangement out of the compartment.

Allow the void disinfected compartment to air dry before use OR wash the unfilled holder with safe water (water that has been dealt with).

Empty, clean water into the disinfected compartment and cover with a tight top.

ELIMINATING AND STORING WATER

Ways to eliminate safe water out of the compartment:

If utilizing a scoop or other gadget, use a clean one each time you eliminate safe water from the storage compartment to help try not to defile the water.

Before scooping out the safe water, make an effort not to contact the water or internal parts of the compartment with your hands.

Never scoop safe water with your hands.

Ways to store safe water in a compartment after cleaning and disinfecting:

Name holder as "drinking water" and incorporate storage date.

Supplant stored water at regular intervals.

Keep stored water in a spot with a cool temperature (50-70°F).

Try not to store water containers in direct daylight.

Try not to store water containers in regions where harmful substances, like fuel or pesticides, are available.

Never use water from unsafe sources.

After an emergency, particularly after flooding, drinking water may not be accessible or safe to drink. Do not use water from radiators or boilers that are important for your home warming framework.

Try not to utilize contaminated well water.

Floods and different debacles can harm drinking water wells and lead to aquifer and well defilement. Floodwater can sully well water with domesticated animal waste, human sewage, synthetic substances, and different impurities that can prompt ailment when utilized for drinking, washing, and other cleanliness exercises. Dug wells, exhausted wells, and different wells under 50 feet deep are bound to be contaminated, even if harm isn't clear.

It is safest to hydrate until you are sure your water is liberated from impurities and safe to drink.

If your water comes from a confidential well that has been overwhelmed, think about the accompanying direction for making water safe and for emergency water sources until you are sure your water is liberated from pollutants and safe to drink.

If broad flooding has happened or you suspect a well might be contaminated, DO NOT hydrate. Utilize a safe water supply like bottled or treated water.

Contact your nearby, state, or ancestral wellbeing office for specific counsel on wells and testing.

Make your water safe to utilize.

Water frequently can be made safe to drink by bubbling, adding sanitizers, or sifting.

Bubble water

Water contaminated with fuel, harmful synthetic compounds, or radioactive material won't be made safe by bubbling or sanitization. Utilize a different wellspring of water if you know or suspect that water may be contaminated with fuel or poisonous synthetics.

If you are suspicious your water is contaminated with fuel or synthetic substances, contact your nearby wellbeing division for specific exhortation.

If you don't have safe bottled water, you ought to bubble water to make it safe. Bubbling is the surest strategy to make water safer to drink by killing illness-causing organic entities, including infections, microorganisms, and parasites.

You can work on the level taste of boiled water by

Pouring it from one clean, sanitized compartment to another and afterward permitting it to represent a couple of hours OR

Adding a touch of salt for every quart or liter of boiled water

Ventures for bubbling shady water

Channel it through a clean material, paper towel, or espresso channel, OR permit it to settle.

Draw off the clear water.

Carry the clear water to a moving bubble for one moment (at rises over 6,500 feet, drop for 3 minutes).

Allow the boiled water to cool.

Store the boiled water in clean, disinfected containers with tight covers.

Ventures for bubbling clear water

Carry the clear water to a moving bubble for one moment (at rises over 6,500 feet, drop for 3 minutes).

Allow the boiled water to cool.

Store the boiled water in clean, disinfected containers with tight covers.

Sanitizers

If you don't have clean, safe bottled water and bubbling is beyond the realm of possibilities, you can frequently make water safer to drink by utilizing a sanitizer, such as unscented family chlorine fade iodine or chlorine dioxide tablets. These can kill the most hurtful organic entities, for example, infections and microbes. Nonetheless, just chlorine dioxide tablets are compelling in controlling more safe living beings, like the parasite Cryptosporidium. If the water is contaminated with a compound, adding a sanitizer won't make it safe to drink.

To sanitize water utilizing bleach:

Bleach comes in different fixations. Ensure you know the grouping of bleach you are utilizing before utilizing it to clean drinking water. It ought to be on the name. Commonly, unscented family fluid chlorine fade in the United States will be somewhere between 5% and 9% sodium hypochlorite, though fixations can be different in different nations.

If your water is shady, channel water through a clean fabric, paper towel, or espresso channel, OR permit it to settle, then draw off the clear water and follow the means beneath.

If your water is clear,

Adhere to the guidelines on the detergent mark for sanitizing drinking water.

If the fundamental directions are not given, add somewhat less than 1/8 teaspoon (8 drops or around 0.5 milliliters) dye for every gallon of clear water (or 2 drops of fade for every liter or every quart of clear water).

Mix the combination well.

Allow it to represent somewhere around 30 minutes prior to utilizing.

Store the sanitized water in clean, disinfected containers with tight covers.

To sanitize water to control for safe organic entities utilizing chlorine dioxide tablets:

Adhere to the producer's guidelines.

Store the cleaned water in clean, disinfected containers with tight covers.

Filters

Numerous versatile water filters can eliminate sickness-causing parasites like Cryptosporidium and Giardia from drinking water.

If you are picking a convenient water channel, attempt to pick one that has a channel pore size sufficiently little to eliminate both microbes and parasites (outright pore size of 1 micron or less). Most convenient water filters don't eliminate microbes or infections.

Painstakingly read and adhere to the producer's guidelines for the water channel. After separating, add a sanitizer like iodine, chlorine, or chlorine dioxide to the sifted water to kill any infections and remaining microbes.

Where to find safe water sources

Elective wellsprings of clean water can be seen inside and outside the home. Try not to DRINK water that has an uncommon smell or variety or that you know or think may be contaminated with fuel or harmful synthetic compounds; utilize a different wellspring of water.

Conceivable home water sources:

Water from your home's water warmer tank (some portion of your drinking water framework, not your home warming framework)

Liquefied ice shapes made with water that was not contaminated

Water from your home's latrine tank (not from the bowl), if it is clear and has not been artificially treated with latrine cleaners like those that change the shade of the water.

Fluid from canned plants

Water from pools and spas that haven't been contaminated with floodwater or stormwater can be utilized for individual cleanliness, cleaning, and related uses. Try not to hydrate from pools or spas.

Pay attention to reports from neighborhood authorities for exhortation on water safeguards in your home.

Conceivable water sources outside the home:

Floodwater can debase well water and streams, streams, and lakes with animal waste, human sewage, synthetics, and other impurities that can prompt sickness when utilized for drinking, washing, and other cleanliness exercises.

Water from sources outside the home should be treated through bubbling, adding sanitizers, or utilizing filters, because it very well may be contaminated with domesticated animal waste or human sewage. If you suspect or know the water is contaminated with harmful synthetic compounds or powers, it can't be made safe. You shouldn't drink or wash in this water.

Potential wellsprings of water that could be caused safe by treatment to incorporate

- Rainwater
- Streams, streams, and other moving waterways
- Lakes and lakes
- Regular springs

Other Methods

- Bright Light (UV Light)
- UV light on water
- Bright light (UV light) can be utilized to kill a few microbes.

Compact units that convey a deliberate portion of UV light help sanitize limited quantities of clear water. UV light doesn't function admirably on cloudy water because little particles might obstruct microbes from the light.

If the water is shady, initial channel it through a clean fabric, paper towel, or espresso channel OR permit it to settle. Then, draw off the clear water and clean it utilizing UV light.

Continuously adhere to the maker's directions.

Sun-based Disinfection

In crises, the sun's beams can work on the nature of water. This technique might lessen a few microorganisms in the water.

To clean water utilizing the sun:

Fill clean and clear plastic jugs with clear water. Sun-oriented sanitization isn't as compelling on cloudy water because little particles might hinder microorganisms from the light.

If the water is shady, initial channel it through a clean fabric, paper towel, or espresso channel OR permit it to settle. Then, at that point, draw off the clear water and sanitize that water utilizing the sun.

Lay the containers down their ally and in the sun for 6 hours (if radiant) or two days (if cloudy). Setting out the containers permits the sun's beams to clean the water inside more successfully.

Putting the jugs on a dim surface will likewise help the sun's beams clean the water all the more real.

WHAT ARE ALL PRECAUTIONS NEEDED TO GET CLEAN WATER/WHAT SHOULD MY EMERGENCY PREPAREDNESS KIT INCLUDE TO ADDRESS MY DRINKING WATER NEEDS?

Water: bottled water, regular water, or another wellspring of clean drinking water.

Food-grade holder to store water (if not utilizing bottled water).

Unscented fluid family chlorine (5-6%) bleach to disinfect water storage compartment (if not utilizing bottled water).

You ought to likewise remember supplies and guidelines for emergency water treatment in case you run out of your stored water. There are a few strategies for treating your water, so make sure to incorporate the things required for the strategy you intend to utilize.

BUBBLING WATER

- Supplies to bubble water (ex: camp oven, fuel, etc.).
- Sanitization
- Unscented fluid family chlorine (5-6%) bleach.
- Filtration
- Convenient water filtration unit, normally accessible at brandishing great stores or anyplace that conveys setting up camp supplies.

HOW MUCH WATER DO I NEED?

You ought to store no less than one gallon of water for every individual each day for at least five days. Individual necessities shift contingent upon age, wellbeing, state of being, movement, diet, and environment.

To decide your water needs, consider the accompanying:

Kids, nursing moms, and sick people might require more water.

A health-related emergency could require extra water.

If you dwell in a warm climate, more water might be essential. In exceptionally hot temperatures, water requirements can be twofold.

Make sure to represent pets; canines and felines ordinarily need 1 gallon each day.

HOW COULD I STORE WATER?

Cautiously putting away your water is important in protecting your water drink.

Notice the termination date for store-purchased water; supplant other stored water at regular intervals.

For bottled water, keep it in its unique compartment and don't open it until you really need to utilize it.

For regular water you have stored in containers, clearly mark the compartment as "drinking water" and incorporate the storage date.

Keep stored water in an area with cool temperatures.

Try not to store containers in direct daylight.

Try not to store water containers in regions where harmful substances, for example, gas or pesticides, are available.

WATER CONTAINERS - KEEP YOUR CLEAN WATER CLEAN!

If you are not involved financially in bottled water for your emergency readiness unit, use food-grade water storage containers (for example, those found at setting up camp stock stores).

Before loading up with safe water, utilize these means to clean and disinfect storage containers:

Wash the storage holder with dishwashing cleanser and water and flush totally with clean water.

Disinfect the compartment by adding an answer made by blending one teaspoon of unscented fluid family chlorine bleach in one quart of water.

Cover the holder and shake it well to ensure that the disinfecting fade arrangement generally contacts the inside surfaces of the compartment.

Stand by something like 30 seconds, and afterward, spill the cleaning arrangement out of the compartment.

Allow the void disinfected holder to air dry before use OR wash the vacant compartment with clean, safe water that is accessible.

Abstain from utilizing the accompanying containers to store safe water:

- Containers that can't be fixed firmly
- Containers that can break, for example, glass bottles
- Containers that have at any point been utilized for any harmful strong or fluid synthetic substances (incorporates old dye containers)
- Plastic or cardboard containers, containers, and containers used for milk or natural product juices

FINDING AN EMERGENCY WATER SOURCE

If you run out of your stored safe drinking water and there could be no other dependable, clean water sources, it might become essential in an emergency to treat water so it is safe to utilize. Treat all water of questionable quality before involving it for drinking, food washing or arrangement, washing dishes, cleaning teeth, or making ice. As well as having a terrible scent and taste, contaminated water can contain microorganisms that can cause infections. Water can be made safe to drink by bubbling, adding sanitizers, or separating.

Significant: Water contaminated with fuel or harmful synthetic substances won't be made safe by bubbling or sterilizations. Utilize a different wellspring of water if you know or suspect that water may be contaminated with fuel or poisonous synthetics.

INSIDE THE HOME

Liquefied ice made with water that was not contaminated.

Fluid from canned plants.

Water from your home's water radiator tank. To utilize this water, be sure the power or gas is off and open the channel at the lower part of the tank. Begin the water streaming by switching off the water consumption esteem at the tank and turning on the hot-water fixture. After you are notified that clean water has been restored, you should top off the tank before turning on the gas or power back on. If the gas is switched off, an expert will be expected to walk out on.

If you get timely notification of a likely fiasco (ex: climate event), you can fill baths or potentially sinks (stay away from utility sinks) before the event as an emergency source if your stored water supply runs out.

Pay attention to reports from nearby authorities for counsel on water safeguards in your home. It could be essential to stop the fundamental water valve in your home to prevent foreign substances from entering your channeling framework.

OUTSIDE THE HOME

Water from sources outside the home should be dealt with.

Rainwater

Streams, streams, and other moving waterways

Lakes and lakes

Normal springs

Try not to DRINK water that has an uncommon smell or variety or that you know or think may be contaminated with fuel or harmful synthetic substances; utilize a different wellspring of water.

UNSAFE SOURCES

Radiators, high temp water boilers (home warming frameworks).

Water from latrine bowl.

Water beds. Fungicides added to the water or synthetic substances in the vinyl might make water unsafe to utilize.

Pools and spas. Synthetic compounds used to kill microbes are excessively focused on safe drinking yet can be utilized for individual cleanliness, cleaning, and related uses.

EMERGENCY TREATMENT OF DRINKING WATER

Whenever you've chosen your wellspring of water, you should treat it before involving it in drinking, food washing or planning, washing dishes, cleaning teeth, or making ice. Water can be purified for drinking by bubbling, adding sanitizers, or sifting.

Significant: Water contaminated with fuel or harmful synthetic substances won't be made safe by bubbling or sterilizations. Utilize a different wellspring of water if you know or suspect that water may be contaminated with fuel or poisonous synthetic substances.

BUBBLING

If you don't have safe bottled water, you ought to bubble water to make it safe. Bubbling is the surest technique to make water safer to drink by killing sickness-causing organic entities, including infections, microbes, and parasites.

You can work on the level taste of boiled water by pouring it starting with one compartment then onto the next and afterward permitting it to represent a couple of hours, OR by adding a spot of salt for every quart or liter of boiled water.

If the water is shady:

Channel it through a clean material, paper towel, or espresso channel

Or permit it to settle, then, at that point, draw off the clear water.

Carry the clear water to a moving bubble briefly (at heights over 6,500 feet, drop for three minutes).

Allow the boiled water to cool.

Store the boiled water in clean, disinfected containers with tight covers.

If the water is clear,

Carry the clear water to a moving bubble briefly (at heights over 6,500 feet, drop for three minutes).

Allow the boiled water to cool.

Store the boiled water in clean, disinfected containers with tight covers.

69

If you don't have safe water and bubbling is unimaginable, you can frequently make water safe to drink by utilizing a sanitizer, such as unscented family chlorine fade or iodine. These can kill most severe life forms, for example, infections and microbes; however, they are not as powerful in controlling more safe living beings like the parasites Cryptosporidium and Giardia.

To clean water:

Channel it through a clean material, paper towel, or espresso channel

Or then again, permit it to settle. Draw off the clear water.

To utilize bleach, add 1/8 teaspoon (or eight drops; around 0.625 milliliters) of unscented fluid family chlorine (5-6%) dye for every gallon of clear water (or two drops of dye for every liter or every quart of water),

Mix the blend well.

Allow it to represent 30 minutes or longer before you use it.

Store the cleaned water in clean, disinfected containers with tight covers.

To utilize iodine, adhere to the producer's directions.

Chlorine dioxide tablets are another sanitizer accessible in a few open-air stores. This sanitizer has been demonstrated to be powerful against microorganisms if the maker's directions are followed.

FILTERS

Numerous compact water filters can eliminate illness-causing parasites like Cryptosporidium and Giardia from drinking water. If you are picking a convenient water channel, attempt to pick one that has a channel pore size sufficiently small to eliminate both microorganisms and parasites. Most versatile water filters don't eliminate infections.

Painstakingly read and adhere to the maker's directions for the water channel you expect to utilize. After separating, add a sanitizer like iodine, chlorine, or chlorine dioxide to the sifted water to kill any infections and remaining microorganisms.

Permit individuals to drink as indicated by their requirements - many individuals need even more than the average of one gallon each day. The singular sum required relies upon age, actual work, state of being, and season.

Never apportion drinking water unless arranged to do as such by specialists - drink the sum you really need today and attempt to track down something else for later. By no means should an individual beverage be short of what one quart (4 cups) of water every day? You can limit how much water your body needs by lessening movement and remaining cool.

Try not to drink carbonated refreshments as opposed to drinking water. Carbonated refreshments don't meet drinking water necessities. Charged beverages and liquor dry out the body, which expands the requirement for drinking water.

Realize where the water admission valve to your house is. If you hear about broken water or sewage lines, you'll have to stop water to your home to avoid allowing contaminated water to enter your home. Pay attention to neighborhood alerts for additional directions. Be sure you and your relatives know how to carry out this significant methodology.

BOOK 5: HOW TO SET UP AND STORE FOOD RESERVES

WHAT TO KEEP IN THE PANTRY AND HOW TO RECYCLE THE STORAGE

Figuring out how to store food for a long has helped individuals for quite a long time, starting with families who had storage spaces or larders. In those days, long-term food storage was a need, as it was the best way to keep dinners new without refrigeration like we have today.

In present-day culture, planning food for long-term storage can be an excellent method for endurance during crises. It is energetically suggested that each family consider having a sufficient stockpile set to the side to keep going for a couple of months.

Begin with an objective of having a multi-month supply of foods you routinely appreciate.

If you have forever been interested in having your own food storeroom with enough holds for your family and an adequate measure of additional items, this guide will be vital to you.

HOW LONG CAN YOU STORE FOOD?

It's vital to know how long you can store food appropriately. Food can be stored for different time spans, contingent upon what you have decided to add to your reserve.

Some food things, like dry beans and white rice, will endure significantly longer than new greens. This is particularly obvious if you expect that you will not approach refrigeration in an emergency.

The essential target of getting all of the ideal foods for long-term storage is to think about their best-by dates. What's more, you need to consider the different ways of helping them keep going significantly longer than on a supermarket rack.

You will track down foods that last as long as 90 days, though others can stay palatable for a really long time. This is fundamental for mortgage holders who need to accumulate sufficient long-term food storage.

If you're picking more medium-term storage, ordinarily as long as 90 days, you can zero in additional on fulfilling and ameliorating dinners as opposed to foods loaded with fundamental nutrients and minerals.

Long-term food storage is intended to keep going for a really long time. These incorporate fixings with a period of usability of 25 years for however long they are appropriately bundled.

FOR HOW LONG CAN FOOD BE STORED IN THE FRIDGE?

The comfort of approaching a cooler during an emergency would be incomprehensibly helpful, particularly as there's no assurance when your power will go out. Nonetheless, only one out of every odd family is keen on planning for endurance. They might be just interested with regards to how long their #1 foods can last when refrigerated.

To guarantee you don't make yourself sick with destructive microorganisms, we utilized graphs to look into the refrigerated lifespan of most foods.

Refrigerated at 40°F or underneath

Food Type	Refrigeration Period
Crude Pork	3 to 5 days
Crude Poultry	1 to 2 days
Crude Beef	1 to 2 days
Soups and Stews	3 to 4 days
Eggs	3 to 5 weeks
Leftovers	3 to 4 days
Lunch Meats	2 weeks (unopened)

Frozen at 0°F or beneath

Food Type	Frozen Period
Crude Pork	4 to a year
Crude Poultry	1 year
Crude Beef	3 to 4 months (ground), 4 to a year (steaks)
Soup and Stews	2 to 90 days
Eggs	Do not freeze
Leftovers	2 to a half-year
Lunch Meats	1 to 2 months

WHAT IS THE IDEAL SURVIVAL FOOD WITH LONG SHELF LIFE?

When you start to investigate endurance foods with the most expanded period of usability, you'll observe a comprehensive combination of things that you can put resources into that will last a significant period.

So, the most pivotal part of protecting food to eat is to guarantee it is fittingly stored. If not, it will spoil rapidly. The best endurance food with the most broadened timeframe of realistic usability is dried beans and rice. When rice and beans are stored appropriately, they can endure as long as 30 years.

The ideal way to ensure your rice and beans remain new and food-safe will be to place them in impermeable containers that help prevent the development of dampness, which is liable for spoiling foods after some time.

You can find a grouping of endurance food producers that will transport beans to you in pre-fixed sealed containers, so you will not need to put resources into specific hardware alone.

Likewise, you can ensure that beans can make an incredible dinner when matched with the right flavors.

WHAT FOODS SHOULD I STOCKPILE FOR SURVIVAL?

Besides rice and beans, you should have a lot of different kinds of food in your drawn-out storage, as you will require a lot of nutrients and minerals to support yourself over the long term.

Food security will let a great deal free from pressure. A few of the other most noteworthy prescribed foods to have in your storage space include:

1. DELICATE GRAINS

Things like corn meal, grain, quinoa, and rye offer undeniably more than making a delectable breakfast. They additionally give as long as eight years of food-safe storage when appropriately fixed.

It is basic that oxygen safeguards are added to the containers and fixed; in any case, they are probably going to spoil. Commonly, it's ideal to buy delicate grains in a sealed shut compartment from the maker straightforwardly.

2. HARD GRAINS

One more grain to look out for is hard grains, like white wheat, millet, and buckwheat. They can be utilized for a grouping of easy-to-understand recipes immediately. Not at all like delicate grains, hard grains can endure significantly longer (as long as 12 years) with legitimate storage.

3. FLOUR

During a highly sensitive situation or a cataclysmic event, one of the primary things that take off your supermarket's racks is flour, basically because it's one of the most multi-reason fixings that is likewise reasonable.

Luckily, flour has a wonderful timeframe of realistic usability of as long as 25 years, for however long it is unground. Preferably, you will need to have the proper hardware to ground the flour on an on-request premise, guaranteeing it has its greatest period of usability.

You will likewise need to ensure that it is stored in a fixed bundle with an oxygen safeguard.

4. DRY PASTA

A thrilling element of dry pasta is that it can possibly endure significantly longer than you'd naturally suspect, particularly if you're somebody who commonly goes by the best-before dates on bundling.

Most sorts of dry pasta at your nearby merchant will endure as long as two years past its expiry date, making it a brilliant choice for making consoling dinners when there's no other option. By and large, pasta can endure as long as 30 years, which is comparable to beans and rice, mainly if it's kept in an impermeable holder. Think about a few assortments, including entire wheat pasta.

5. CANNED BEANS

If you would prefer to zero in fundamentally on canned foods for a medium-term storage arrangement, canned beans can be an extraordinary option compared to dried ones. You can anticipate that most canned beans should endure as long as six years for however long they are stored in a cool and dry spot. Quite possibly, the main thing while canning foods is to think about botulism, as it very well may be destructive.

6. GET DRIED-OUT FRUITS AND VEGETABLES

More property holders are putting resources into dehydrators because they are generally simple to utilize and are an extraordinary method for making your own dried natural products to nibble on over time.

You'll have an assortment of choices to dry out. They can give truly necessary calories in emergency circumstances.

Be that as it may, a dehydrator can likewise be a priceless asset with regard to preparing for an emergency. You can dry out apples, raisins, apricots, and more to help them last as long as 30 years suitably stored.

Likewise, with some other sort of food that you have stored, you should routinely check for indications of deterioration, which can introduce itself as a foul smell, overflowing, or shape.

Long-term food storage organizations will likewise have a broad rundown of dried-out natural products to look over that show pre-bundled and with dampness safeguards.

Within a similar classification, you can pick to purchase or make dried-out vegetables to help guarantee you and your family can get adequate nutrients and minerals for as long as 20 years.

7. DRIED OR FREEZE-DRIED MEATS

If you didn't approach refrigeration during an emergency, you probably wouldn't get by eating meat because it spoils somewhat rapidly when stored at temperatures above 40°F. A fabulous option is to settle on dried meats, with store-purchased assortments enduring two years if the bundling stays unopened.

An even improved arrangement is to make your own. Guarantee that you utilize lean meats, though, as they will endure significantly longer than fatty cuts.

Restoring meats is specialty expertise; however, it is phenomenal expertise to have available to you to ensure you don't need to do without the essential proteins from a portion of your #1 type of meat.

You will likewise be answerable for ensuring you have the appropriate bundling to prevent oxygen from penetrating the seal and ensuring the meat is stored away from daylight.

Freeze-dried meat is one more famous other option, as it ensures that your meat will remain safe for as long as 15 years when stored appropriately.

8. CANNED MEAT

There are different canned meat you can find at the supermarket. Canned meat can surrender you to five years of food supplies as long as you guarantee to look at them for botulism before eating.

When you begin investigating canned meats for your stores, you'll need to pick recipes with two fundamental fixings: meat and salt. Any other way, they could spoil quicker and simply offer as long as two years of the period of usability.

9. PEANUT BUTTER

As a fundamental for most individuals' morning meals, peanut butter is a phenomenal fix because of its high-fat substance. It's additionally high in calories. It is delicious when you pair it with a variety of dinners.

You'll love to know that rather than the ordinary containers of pre-made spread that you find at the supermarket, you can likewise decide on powdered peanut butter, which will endure significantly longer and can be utilized on an on-request premise.

Powdered peanut butter has as long as 15 years of a timeframe of realistic usability contrasted with as long as two years of a time of usability that you'd get with pre-blended groups.

10. SUGARS AND SWEETENERS

You'll love to know there are a lot of sugars and regular sugars that can endure endlessly in your food storage, like wild honey. You should store these fixings with care. For instance, wild honey can be spoiled if it is presented to water, so it should be in a dampness-resistant compartment.

Another incredible option is white sugar, earthy colored sugar, powdered, or pure sweetener, which can likewise be stored endlessly when airtight fixed.

Unadulterated maple syrup is a well-known decision among survivalists. Maple syrup can add a ton to recipes, like sugar-coated bacon, yet you should ensure the brand you are purchasing is 100 percent pure maple syrup.

Sadly, many of the well-known staples purchased brands don't contain maple syrup in their fixings. The equivalent can be said about corn syrup, whether the container has been opened or stayed fixed.

11. POWDERED MILK

Another immense essence that will probably be sold out in any store during an emergency is powdered milk. This is because powdered milk can endure as long as 25 years if you store it in a cool and dry area.

One of the most extensive advantages of this choice is that it's not difficult to tell when it has turned sour, as it will go to a yellow tone and smell foul.

12. FLAVORS AND SPICES

Any sort of preparing that you have ought to be dry, if conceivable. Overall, most flavors and flavors can endure as long as four years, contingent upon how you store them.

13. MRES

Although they can be more expensive than different kinds of endurance food, MREs appears to be one of the most well-known decisions for individuals who need speedy in a hurry suppers that are not difficult to assemble.

There are a lot of different recipes that you can find, going from chicken teriyaki to macaroni and cheddar. They are inconceivably advantageous because they accompany an onboard cooking arrangement.

By following a couple of steps on the rear of the bundling, you can plan hot dinners matched with dessert right away. The main issue with MREs is that their timeframe of realistic usability will fluctuate radically, contingent upon where you get them from.

A few makers have MREs that can endure as long as 30 years, though others may simply endure as long as ten years. Perusing the item depiction before buying is fundamental. Some have noticed that they are not the most lovely dinners on the planet.

Nonetheless, they are loaded with nutrients and minerals to give you delayed essentialness in an emergency, including cataclysmic events. They are ideal emergency food proportions.

14. JARS OF VEGETABLES

Canned vegetables are choices if you use them by the "utilization by" date. This can be 1 - 5 years, contingent upon what it is and where you get it from. Acidic foods won't keep going as long as non-acidic. This is something to load up on when they are discounted, pivot, and afterward, recharge.

WHAT IS NEEDED TO STORE SURVIVAL FOOD?

Taking into account that buying food from emergency food providers can be pricey, it will probably be more financially savvy to bundle your emergency supplies at home. For this, you'd need to ensure that you have the appropriate bundling devices.

Sealed shut containers are fundamental. You can involve them in a wide range of food.

Not exclusively will you need to make sure that you have things that can be airtight fixed; however, you likewise have an assortment of oxygen safeguards to help prevent your food from spoiling.

Perhaps the savviest answer for putting away huge and little amounts of dried foods is the utilization of mylar sacks, particularly as you can get them in mass at somewhat low costs.

Anticipating food storage when everything goes wrong/when disaster strikes

Mylar sacks for food storage are normally made from food-safe foil. They help to hinder oxygen and light from infiltrating your food, making it spoil early.

They are not appropriate for those who need to shield their food from rodents, as plastic sacks are unimaginably simple to bite through. An all the more tough choice could be food-safe plastic pails. Food-grade containers can help foods last as long as 30 years when stored in ideal circumstances.

Aside from the sort of bundling you pick, you will likewise need to ensure your storage space is helpful and safe for ideal food security.

Aside from the sort of bundling you pick, you will likewise need to ensure your storage room is helpful and safe for ideal food insurance.

It should be a cool and dry area that doesn't depend on HVAC to be temperature-controlled, which is why cold basements or underground storerooms are number one among preppers. Also, a cooler is great; however, if you don't have electricity, all that will eventually spoil.

It's additionally crucial to ensure there aren't any wellsprings of light that could influence your bundling. If conceivable, decide on a room that doesn't have windows. Think about building a root basement.

WHAT QUANTITY OF FOOD SHOULD I STORE FOR A LONG PERIOD?

Preparing is for everybody. When choosing how much food to have for an emergency, the things you will need to consider first are the following:

Number of individuals you plan on taking care of

Time allotment you need to plan for

The amount of room you possess to store it

These two variables can significantly influence how much food you'll have to buy to ensure you have enough for your friends and family.

You will likewise need to consider whether you'll be a decent Samaritan and give a portion of your food stores to your neighbors, or on the other hand, if you expect to segregate yourself away from the overall population.

Regarding food, in any event, each home ought to have as long as seven days' worth for every family to eat three dinners each day, with snacks; however, that is the exceptionally least.

You will need to consider the time span you need to get ready for and change your proportions as required.

Clean Water

While enough calories each day are significant, drying out will be a more prompt worry than starvation in an emergency. Having a stockpile of clean water ought to be your first concern. This is particularly significant if you have exceptionally dynamic individuals in your family that will have a rundown of obligations to take care of.

You will likewise need to consider your current circumstance. Sweltering environments will expect people to have more water than cold temperatures. This is valid for dry environments also.

It's additionally fundamental to have sufficient clean water to stay aware of food readiness and cleanliness. You won't need relatives becoming sick because of inappropriate cleanliness.

You need to have a fourteen-day supply of water for every relative, as proposed by FEMA, with one gallon of water for each individual each day.

STEP-BY-STEP INSTRUCTIONS TO STORE FOOD LONG TERM

While you're sorting out some way to store food for long and arranging your emergency food supply, there are a lot of steps to take to guarantee you're making the most out of your time and cash. Safety is vital.

While purchasing mass foods, many individuals consider canned vegetables, white rice, and dry beans, yet there are extra simple to-store foods like an assortment of freeze-dried foods and dried-out foods. Recollect likewise, add-water dinners.

You can have a few sorts of food that last as long as 30 years with good storage. While not an endless timeframe of realistic usability, it is a brilliant food storage plan when thoroughly examined.

This will ensure your family is adequately shrouded in an emergency. Having an assortment of food likewise implies you can turn and recharge it.

SAFEGUARDING/PROTECTING YOUR PRESERVED FOOD OVER TIME FROM MOLD AND BACTERIA AND HOW TO STOCKPILE FOOD USING CANNING, FREEZING, DEHYDRATING, PICKLING, AND OTHER TECHNIQUES AND STORE FOOD FOR WEEKS, MONTHS, AND YEARS

To expand the life span of food utilized at home, you can use refrigeration, freezing, canning, sugaring, salting, and even vacuum pressing. Besides, food specialists continually explore new conservation techniques to grow our choices.

Hundreds of years of experimentation have shown us the safest strategies for food safeguarding, which you should focus on if you need to hold the quality and cleanliness of stored food. Fortunately, with the right direction and materials, you can undoubtedly do such in any setting.

THE IMPORTANCE OF FOOD PRESERVATION

Food preservation refers to the cycles you use to get ready food for safe, long-time storage, whether you intend to utilize it at home, prep in a business kitchen, or sell straightforwardly to buyers. Conservation techniques help hinder bacterial development and different kinds of waste, meaning the food is safe and fulfilling to eat from now on.

There are three motivations behind why food conservation is significant:

To limit pathogenic microscopic organisms - food in long-term storage is at serious gamble of decay because of microorganisms like E. coli, Salmonella, and different microorganisms. Microorganisms need warmth, dampness, and time to duplicate food quickly, yet food conservation hinders at least one of these circumstances and stops their development. To preserve food at its best quality - Food falls apart over the long run because of deterioration. Generally speaking, gentle decay doesn't make food unsafe to eat, yet it significantly influences its taste, surface, and appearance. Appropriate food safeguarding can help hold a portion of these characteristics and the healthy benefit of specific foods.

To set aside cash - to waste is expensive, both at home and in a business setting. In a perfect world, you ought to try not to purchase beyond what you can utilize, yet different protection strategies - if done safely - help you keep vegetables, natural products, meat, and so on far beyond their standard lapse, so there's compelling reason need to receptacle them.

Certain food conservation techniques can be interesting, yet odds are you'll acquire a genuine feeling of fulfillment and pride when you effectively apply them. Additionally, as numerous safeguarding techniques require accuracy and mind to keep up with food safety, you'll reinforce your consciousness of food cleanliness dangers and great practices.

STANDARD METHODS OF FOOD PRESERVATION

Food conservation strategies range from the straightforward course of chilling to additional mind-boggling methodology, for example, canning. Many are imaginative choices that help you stir things up at home or sell food in different types of bundling. Others allow you to save your stock in a business kitchen, which implies you lessen waste and increase profit.

The six segments underneath take a gander at different food protection strategies you can utilize and the safest, best method for doing them.

CHILLING

Although refrigeration is a fundamental storage strategy nowadays, it was once an extravagance. Putting away food at a low temperature is the least complex and frequently safest method for putting away many sorts of food.

Refrigerators save the quality and safety of food because the virus eases back bacterial development and limits waste. Contingent upon the sort of food, it can endure between a couple of days and half a month in the cooler before the surface and taste break down.

Fridges save the quality and security of food because the virus eases back bacterial development and limits decay. Contingent upon the kind of food, it can endure between a couple of days and half a month in the fridge before the surface and taste decay.

To securely refrigerate food, you ought to:

Set your fridge to a temperature somewhere in the range of 1°C and 4°C. The law expects you to store food for business use under 8°C.

Utilize separate coolers, where conceivable, for a crude and high gamble or prepared to-eat food to limit cross-pollution. If it's unconventional for you to utilize separate fridges, you ought to know which fridge racks you should store food on. For instance, prepared to-eat food ought to sit above crude food consistently.

Ensure you mark food with best previously and use by dates if you eliminate the first packaging.

Abstain from over-burdening the fridge or putting food before the cooling unit. Guarantee there's a lot of room between foods to permit airflow.

Put canned food in a different compartment before you refrigerate it. When you refrigerate any open can, a limited quantity of metal exchanges to the food, which, although not destructive to utilization, gives food an unappetizing taste.

Utilize a FIFO food capacity framework to guarantee you utilize those with the closest best previously or use by dates before others. A legitimate stock revolution limits waste and sets aside your cash.

Did you know?

Throughout history, different civilizations cut and stored ice or snow to make conditions for refrigeration. Ice was even transported all over the planet.

If stored appropriately, frozen food can keep going for a really long time. Because microbes can't develop when frozen, the food you save in the cooler can stay to eat for practically endless timeframes. Notwithstanding, it will eventually crumble in quality and become unappetizing, so you should utilize most frozen food within a couple of months or a year.

To securely freeze food, you ought to:

Set the cooler to a temperature between - 18°C and - 22°C.

Place food in impermeable compartments or cooler bags before freezing. Appropriate wrapping is particularly significant for meat; any other way, it might get cooler to consume and become unpalatable.

Just freeze things before their best previously or use them by date.

Never refreeze thawed-out food, as it offers microorganisms a chance to develop between defrosting. You should either utilize it immediately or store it in the fridge for as long as 24 hours.

Thaw out the cooler routinely to keep it liberated from a block of ice developing. It's advisable to save frozen food in the fridge for two or three hours greatest while the cooler thaws out.

Name food with the date you put it inside the fridge so you can refer back to the date to see whether you should utilize the food before it breaks down.

Did you know?

If the power cuts, don't open the cooler entryway. For the most part, food stays frozen for about 24 hours even if the cooler stops, so you don't need to discard anything once the power returns.

Saving food in a high-sugar climate stops bacterial development by diminishing the food's water content. It functions admirably for organic products: you can make jam and jelly that goes on for quite a while, and you can utilize canning to store it (see the part underneath).

A wide range of sweet substances functions admirably to protect food, including sugar granules, sugar syrup, or honey. Some sugaring recipes even use liquor close by sugar to safeguard specific foods.

You might utilize sugaring to safeguard foods, for example,

Organic products - apples, peaches, plums, apricots, cherries, and more save well when sugared.

Vegetables - ginger and carrot are generally sugared and utilized for relishes or toppings.

For certain fish and meat - you can consolidate sugar with salt or one more fluid to make brackish water that helps safeguard meat and decrease pungency.

Utilizing an over-the-top measure of sugar accompanies well-being gambles, yet if you diminish how much sugar to lower than what is needed, you might permit the food to spoil. Make sure you follow appropriate sugaring recipes shared on the web or in books to get the perfect sum and make sure to eat sugared foods with some restraint.

Did you know?

The typical individual consumes 24 kilos of sugar a year: six times the suggested sum.

SALTING

Like sugaring, salt coaxes water out of food and stops bacterial development. At a high point, it might eradicate microscopic organisms' cells, although the food is logical unappetizing by this point.

There are two types of salting:

Dry restoring - you apply salt to the food, like meat, and pass on it to draw out the water.

Wet restoring - otherwise called saline solution, you blend salt in with water and add food to the fluid to safeguard it, normally along with canning.

Likewise, over-the-top salt utilization can hurt well-being with sugar, so you ought to follow reasonable salting recipes found on the web or in distributed food safeguarding books. You likewise need to utilize salt specifically intended for pickling or Kosher salt.

CANNING

Keeping food canned significantly expands its lifespan provided it's done accurately. The canning system jelly food by eliminating oxygen through an impermeable seal and containing food in an acidic, sweet, or pungent climate, where microbes can't flourish.

You ought to follow a protected, legitimate canning process:

Select excellent quality food that is still within its best previously or use by date. Handle it cleanly.

Buy appropriate containers and self-fixing covers specifically intended for canning. You can't reuse old peanut butter containers and jam pots; they will not guarantee an impermeable seal.

Buy a canning rack.

Follow tried protection recipes. You should follow each progression cautiously to make sure your canned foods save securely.

Follow these canning steps:

Heat the containers in advance in stewing water (not bubbling).

Set up the food as indicated by the protection recipe. You ordinarily need to warm food to bubble.

Eliminate containers from the water and freely fill them with the food.

Contingent upon the recipe, you might fill the container with the food (for example, jam), or you might have to add an acidic fluid or salt water, which you'll bubble ahead of time.

Leave ½ inch of headspace and apply the fixing cover. Change the top until the fit is fingertip tight.

Lower the containers in bubbling water utilizing your canning rack for the recipe's timeframe.

Eliminate and save for cooling however long expressed.

You must follow a tried canning interaction to expand food's life span and security. If inappropriately canned, food containing C. botulinum might deliver poisons that cause botulism harming: an intriguing, however life-compromising condition. Luckily, C. botulinum stays latent in high-corrosive conditions, so make sure you follow any means that require adding acids.

Did you know?

Because of Napoleon's anxiety about fighters kicking the bucket from hunger, a man named Nicholas Appert created canning in the mid-1800s.

VACUUM PACKING

Like canning, vacuum packing denies microorganisms of oxygen by making impermeable air. While food may not keep going, however long canned products, vacuuming still expands its capacity life any more than keeping food in the fridge or a cabinet.

Vacuum packing likewise has esteem as a conservation strategy because it saves the quality without the requirement for different fixings (dissimilar to canning). It, as a rule, keeps up with the food's smell, variety, taste, and surface - which is especially attractive for meat you expect to cook interesting. Vacuum-packed food likewise holds its dampness, which guarantees ideal food quality without even a trace of air.

Past protection, vacuum packing likewise functions admirably for food readiness. Numerous culinary specialists vacuum pack specific fixings and cook them at an exact temperature to deliver extraordinary outcomes.

To securely vacuum pack food, you ought to:

Set up the food cleanly. Wash leafy foods and trim meat's undesirable skin, fat, and bone.

Place the food inside a reasonable vacuum-packing plastic container.

Then feed the plastic bag into a vacuum packing device.

Permit the vacuum packing machine to run.

Store in the fridge or find a cool, dry spot.

You can follow specific strategies that don't need a machine to vacuum pack food if you like; however, they generally sacrifice food well-being and produce changing outcomes. Keep in mind: to prevent botulism, impenetrable packaging should be right on target. In a business setting, consistently utilize reasonable hardware to vacuum pack. You'll protect food securely and make it protected to eat sometime in the future.

Did you know?

You can vacuum seal a ton of foods; however, you should stay away from mild cheddar, mushrooms, broccoli, cabbage, and Brussels sprouts. They radiate gases that grow in the bag and lead to decay.

HOW TO SALVAGE ADDITIONAL FOOD BASED ON THE ENVIRONMENT SURROUNDING YOUR BUNKER

The vast majority don't understand how much food they discard consistently — from uneaten extras to spoiled produce to parts of plants that could be eaten or reused.

33% of all food in the United States goes uneaten. EPA gauges that in 2018, about 81 percent - 20.3 tons - of families' wasted food wound up in landfills or ignition facilities.

Preventing food from going to waste is one of the most straightforward and most impressive moves you can make to set aside cash and lower your environmental change impression by decreasing ozone-depleting substance (GHG) outflows and preserving average assets.

Ways Of preventing Wasted Food at Home

Arranging, preparing, and putting away food can help your family waste less food. Here are what will help you:

ARRANGING AND SHOPPING TIPS

Creating a rundown in light of weekly meals can set aside your cash and time. If you just purchase what you hope to utilize, you will be bound to keep it new and use everything.

Keep a running rundown of meals and their fixings that your family now appreciates - like that, you can undoubtedly pick, look for, and plan meals that you are probably going to consume.

Search in your fridge, cooler, and storage room first to try not to purchase food you now have. Make a table plan every seven days of what should be spent and plan forthcoming meals around it.

Arrange your meals for the week before you go out to shop and purchase just the things required for those meals.

Make your shopping list in light of the number of meals you'll eat at home. Consider how frequently you will eat out, if you intend to eat frozen pre-cooked meals, and if you will eat extras for any of your meals.

Master amounts for your shopping list, noticing the number of meals you'll make with everything to avoid overbuying. Purchasing in enormous amounts (e.g., get one, get one free arrangement) possibly sets aside cash if you utilize all the food before it spoils.

Purchasing food from mass receptacles can set aside your cash and lessen food waste and packaging as you can buy how much food you want rather than a pre-decided sum. While purchasing in mass, make sure to store food appropriately in hermetically sealed, marked compartments.

Buy flawed produce or upcycled items. Blemished produce might have actual flaws yet is comparably protected and nutritious and can sometimes be found at limited costs. Upcycled items are produced using fixings that could have, in any case, gone to waste.

Appropriately store leafy foods for most extreme newness; they'll taste better and last longer, helping you to eat a greater amount of them before they turn sour.

Most veggies, particularly those that could shrink (like salad greens, carrots, cucumbers, and broccoli), should go in the fridge's high stickiness cabinet.

Most organic products and vegetables that will generally decay (like mushrooms and peppers) ought to go in the low dampness cabinet of the fridge.

A few natural products (like bananas, apples, pears, natural stone products, and avocados) discharge ethylene gas as they age, making other nearby produce mature and possibly spoil quicker. Store these away from other produce.

Hold on to wash berries, cherries, and grapes until you're prepared to eat them to prevent form.

Some products, such as potatoes, eggplant, winter squash, onions, and garlic, should be stored in a cool, dry, dull, and very much ventilated place.

Make sure you are appropriately putting away food in your cooler.

The cooler entryway is the hottest piece of the fridge. You can store sauces there, yet putting away milk or eggs in the door isn't suggested.

The lower racks are the coldest piece of the fridge. Store meat, poultry, and fish here.

Coolers should be set to keep a temperature of 40 °F or underneath.

Store grains in impenetrable compartments and name the holder with the items and the date.

Get to know your cooler and visit it frequently. Freeze food like bread, cut natural products, meat, or extras that you know will not be eaten in time. Name the items and the date.

COOKING AND PREPARATION TIPS

Produce that is over the hill, as well as miscellaneous items of fixings and extras, may, in any case, be fine for cooking. Reuse these fixings in soups, meals, sautés, frittatas, sauces, heated products, flapjacks, or smoothies. You'll try not to waste these things and may even make another most loved dish.

If protected and solid, utilize the consumable pieces of food you typically don't eat. For instance, flatbread can be used to make croutons, beet greens can be sautéed for a flavorful side dish, and vegetable pieces can be utilized for soup stock.

Gain proficiency with the difference between "sell-by," "use-by," "best-by," and termination dates

Mean to cook and serve the right parcels for the number of people you are taking care of.

Freeze, pickle, get dried out, can, or make jam/jam from excess plants - particularly plentiful occasional produce.

Try not to leave transitory food at room temperature for over two hours.

Refrigerate or freeze any extras in little, clear, named compartments with a date.

Tool stash for Your Home and Your Community

The Food: Too Good to the Waste toolkit will help you sort out how much food is genuinely going to waste in your home and how you might waste less. By making little shifts in the way you search for, plan, and store food, you can set aside time and cash. It can likewise keep the important assets used to create and disperse food from going to waste!

DIET AND BUDGET - EASILY ROTATE AND USE YOUR EMERGENCY FOOD SUPPLY, SO NOTHING GOES TO WASTE

Whether you're stressed over an unexpected cutback, home intrusions, fender benders, the power going out for seven days, catastrophic events, or long-term financial and cultural decay, it's essential that you start arrangements now. By definition, if you hold on until you want it, it's now past the point of no return.

You're in good company: Millions of reasonable people from varying backgrounds are viewing readiness in a severe way — and the development is developing as additional people acknowledge they can't rely upon others to save them in our impacting world.

It's basic: contingent upon what occurs, you'll either remain in your home, leave your home, or be away from home. Making it unnecessarily confounded makes you less ready.

Be that as it may, preparing can appear to be overpowering. Furthermore, to make matters more terrible, there's a ton of insane "boisterous minority" garbage out there that dirties judicious readiness with fanaticism, hazardous data, or senseless web discussions that don't make any difference.

The general purpose of preparing is to diminish the possibilities of significant life disturbances and, all the more likely, recuperate from interruptions when they occur. That is all there is to it!

Try not to search for a solitary agenda and skirt the reading. You will save yourself much cash and time and be more ready if you find an opportunity to gain from others as opposed to misstepping the same way most novices make when they attempt to "skirt the vegetables." The primary purpose of preparing well is knowing and following the correct way, not placing a container of stuff in your storage room.

The essential strides to preparing:

Construct a strong individual budget and well-being establishment

Prepare your home for quite some time of independence

Have the option to leave your home with one minute's notification ("bug out bags")

Plan for crises that happen away from home ("return home bags" and regularly convey)

Master center abilities and practice with your stuff

Offer and enroll while proceeding to learn and going past the nuts and bolts

Tips and regular amateur mix-ups

Large numbers of these are sorted through in the normal prepper rules. To feature the most widely recognized:

Try not to pay off-the-rack packs. 98% of them are not worth purchasing.

You can't forecast when an emergency will occur, so a decent prep is dependably prepared.

You can't anticipate what will occur, so be persevering about finding and keeping away from presumptions in your preparation.

Remain sensible and pragmatic. Keep away from zombies and Rambo dreams. Center around the things that make the biggest difference and recall that less complex is better.

Try not to let preparing overpower or overcome you. Partaking in easy street now and not going down a dim winding of Armageddon misery or blowing your life reserve funds on supplies is significant. You can plan without surrendering, like how purchasing health care coverage doesn't mean you've abandoned your well-being.

Disregard the commotion and radicalism that attempts to take over preparing from the edges. Tragically, many connected online journals, discussions, and Facebook bunches are filled with garbage. Shout out or head off to someplace else.

Preparing is better when you associate with similar people. Attempt to interface with others through this site and through nearby gatherings (e.g., scouts, CERT, beginner radio clubs, climbing clubs, etc.)

Stay away from "going in for seconds" your stuff. For instance, it's enticing to select things from your bug-out bag for a setting up camp excursion. However, at that point, life will, in general, disrupt everything, the stuff stays dissipated, and that makes windows where an emergency could strike, and you're ill-equipped.

If you're on a careful spending plan, it's wiser to purchase less top-notch things than modest stuff that will fail when you want them most.

Try not to simply get some stuff, toss it in a storeroom, congratulate yourself, and continue on. You are not arranged unless you practice with your supplies and plans.

A bug-out bag isn't just for bugging out to a foreordained area along a foreordained way. It's the one bag you snatch first when you need to leave your home.

It's inappropriate to think "I will probably bug out" or "I will probably shield set up at home" — crises couldn't care less about your arrangements, and a proper prep implies having the option to do both.

Arrangement in light of your dangers

It's extremely normal in friendly gatherings for people to answer a fledgling prepper's supplication for help by inquiring, "all things considered, what are you preparing for?" and afterward fitting plans and supplies specific to that event.

That isn't horrendous, and it has the advantage of keeping people grounded as opposed to being caught in Judgment daydreams.

In any case, practically speaking, that psychological model makes people get exclusive focus — which then, at that point, makes their prepares less successful or proficient — or sends the mixed signal that there are tremendous differences in how to get ready.

Fortunately, the preparation rudiments schedule is no different for 98% of people and situations.

It's once you move beyond those fundamentals that things begin to get redone or precarious — if you have any desire to grow an indoor nursery in your city studio, for instance, or have uncommon clinical necessities.

There are specifics you layer on top of the essentials relying upon your neighborhood chances. If you're getting ready for a typhoon, for instance, you'd need to sort out your tempest screens plan sooner than later. Be that as it may, all the center stuff like fourteen days of supplies and a go-bag are something very similar.

Maslow's pecking order and the Pareto 80-20 rule

We gossip about the 80-20 rule (the "Pareto standard") on The Prepared and how it should direct emergency readiness.

The underlying 20% of all the conceivable work you could do in preparing gets you 80% of the way there. To go from 80% to 100 percent arranged requires significantly more work and cash.

That guideline applies throughout the preparation. For instance, you should plan for the 80% of likely situations, not the improbable ones like extremist zombies showing up on a radioactive outsider space rock.

Maslow's progressive system is a well-known brain science rule that makes sense of what people need to get by and flourish, arranged by significance:

Prepper agenda needs preparing on a careful spending plan.

The establishment is, clearly, fundamentals like air, water, and sanctuary. Numerous preppers refer to The Rule of 3's: You can endure 3 minutes without air, 3 hours without cover in awful circumstances, 3 days without water, and three weeks without food.

Whenever you take care of them, you can then contemplate the following layer, etc. At the highest point of the pyramid is self-completion, which implies things like getting a charge out of side interests and "tracking down yourself."

Utilize these two basic structures to keep your arrangements grounded and focused. For instance, having four exhausting meals than two of your #1 meals is vastly improved.

In all honesty, we see people committing these errors constantly.

STAGE 1: GET YOUR WELL-BEING AND FUNDS ALL TOGETHER

Clinical issues and monetary difficulties are the possible disturbances you'll look at in your lifetime, and since you're a sensible prepper, you focus on the most probable crises first.

The measurements around personal monetary well-being are amazingly terrible — especially in the US. For instance, more than half of Americans can't deal with a startling

$500 emergency (e.g., your terminated guarantee home heater out of nowhere falls flat) without utilizing Mastercards.

You shouldn't spend any cash on gear/supplies past the fundamentals (e.g., fourteen days of water in your home) without first having center monetary prepares, for example, a windy day store, obligation decrease plan, and retirement reserve funds.

72 hours versus fourteen days

As of not long ago, emergency readiness directs ordinarily suggested having 72 hours' worth of supplies. Being arranged means having your own food, water, and different supplies to keep going for no less than 72 hours.

They're off-base. Making due for 72 hours is better than a kick in the pants than nothing, yet most current specialists accept you should be ready for no less than about fourteen days to deal with most of the likely events.

"There is an earnest requirement for occupants to plan for quite a long time." — said Robert Ezelle

Ongoing events like Hurricane Harvey, the Japanese Tsunami, Haiti Earthquake, and the California Wildfires are instances of restricted fiascos where people were uprooted or without essential administration for weeks.

In 2016 the US Navy, Coast Guard, and Washington state's National Guard did a full-scale, nine-day drill to test how well they could answer a gigantic quake in the Cascadia Subduction Zone. That region covers Vancouver, Seattle, and Portland through northern California.

The 83-page report reaches many unnerving ends. The writers concede the frameworks are not prepared, the foundation would implode, and they'd have an out-and-out philanthropic emergency in ten days.

We evaluated the Portland Water Bureau, and they had a comparative message about a quake around there: 1,000,000 people in that 225-square-mile region will be without water for months, not days.

Legislative issues and planning are compounding the situation after some time, worse. It would require basically seven days to appropriately facilitate outside assets acquired to help. For instance, the American military reports they need eight days to prepare a reaction inside the US line — and that is only for a somewhat confined emergency, like a quake.

STAGE 2: GET YOUR HOME PREPARED FOR A VERY LONG TIME OF CONFIDENCE

We start with the home because it's where you invest the greater part of your energy and is generally the best spot to make it through an emergency. This is why legislatures give the norm "remain in your home!" counsel during an emergency.

Model circumstances:

You have a startling enormous cost or cutback that blows your limited financial plan

School and work are dropped because of a devastating intensity wave

The electrical or water network goes down for a couple of days

A frightful storm floods your city for seven days

A pestilence is spreading, and you're isolated in your home

Common request separates from mass agitation on the roads

A close-by city is gone after by a foe

Absolute breakdown ("Shit Hits The Fan")

You need to get by in your home for fourteen days without external help — whether from people or the matrix. That implies you can't expect to have power, water, cooking or warming gas, correspondence, web, 911, ambulances, etc.

Home agenda synopsis:

Water: store 15 gallons of consumable water per individual (about 1 gallon each day) and have ways of treating grimy water through either a versatile water channel or ledge water channel

Food: no less than 23,000 calories for every individual (about 1,500 calories each day) of stable rack food that is prepared to eat or just necessities bubbling water to make; typically one or a blend of additional store food you regularly eat at any rate or unique prepper food that endures until the end of time

Fire: lighters, matches, and reinforcement fire starters

Light: headlamps, spotlights, candles, lamps

Warming and cooling: indoor-safe radiators, additional covers, USB-controlled fan

Cover: a canvas (even a modest one you find at a neighborhood store) proves to be useful for ad-libbed cover, connecting openings in the house, and clearing trash

Clinical: a rundown of 145 focused on home clinical supplies

Cleanliness: moist disposable clothes, hand sanitizer, camp cleanser

Correspondence: either a one-way NOAA radio or two-way ham radio (if you know how to utilize it)

Power: spare batteries and rechargers (your bug-out bag will have a sunlight-based charger; however, you can likewise get a second one for home)

Apparatuses: hatchet, scoop, work gloves, a wrench for your gas lines, zip ties, pipe tape, etc.

Self-preservation: relies upon individual perspectives, may incorporate defensive body layer, guns, pepper shower, etc.

Cash: however much you can sensibly stand to stash

Emotional wellness: prepackaged games, most loved books, earphones, films downloaded to a tablet, etc.

Reports: duplicate of deeds/titles, insurance contracts, birth certificates, maps, pictures of relatives, and so on in both physical and USB thumb drive structures

Nearby and emergency data: record significant contact numbers, know the area of the closest medical clinics, and so on.

Each amateur ought to comprehend the First In, First Out model ("store what you use, use what you store"). It's a simple method for developing your home supplies without additional expense or exertion and applies to water, food, and everyday consumables like tissue and batteries.

Water is simply too essential to even think about taking a risk with. So don't expect to have the opportunity to fill the bath or race to the store, and don't utilize unseemly vessels, for example, milk containers. Get legitimate water stockpiling tanks.

Food isn't as essential as water since the vast majority can endure a long time without it. In this way, for your crucial transient emergency inclusion, you don't have to ponder "making" food by planting, hunting, etc. The primary line of safeguard is to simply have some other rack of stable food close by. People meet this objective in one of two different ways (or both):

Have extra of the stuff you typically purchase and eat in any case.

Purchase "endurance food" that you won't open until an emergency

The advantage of the store route is that you don't wind up with stuff you may in all likelihood never use, and, in an emergency, you'd continue to eat similar stuff you're utilized to. The disadvantage is that you want more extra room than the endurance food way, and if it's not your ordinary propensity to cook much at home, there's a breaking point on the amount you can store before gambling any waste.

The food you wouldn't air out until an emergency is more costly, yet it takes less space for a similar measure of calories, expects practically no cooking, and can keep going on a rack for 20-30 years.

What is a bug-out bag? Why should I have one?

An emergency can strike whenever. You may just have seconds to leave your home. Or, on the other hand, perhaps you gain a benefit (e.g., beating traffic) by emptying while every other person is as yet scrambling.

That is why a centerpiece of being arranged has one bag that is constantly packed and prepared to utilize — regardless; you'll know you have the right core basics to get by, easily handle the outcome, and possibly help others around you.

So your bug-out bag is your emergency pack since you'll be alright if that is the main thing you at any point have/plan.

Reward: As a fledgling prepper, building your go-bags is in numerous ways equivalent to building an emergency pack for your home. Since the bag is constantly kept at home, if something occurs around the house or you cover set up during a more extended emergency, those go-bag supplies can be utilized if required.

Since you can't expect you'll have vehicle transportation, these bags are intended to be foot convenient. That implies utilizing a backpack and keeping things at a sensible load while thinking about your neighborhood climate.

A few people think a bug-out bag is solely for "bugging out" along a foreordained way to a pre-supplied "bug-out area" (like a lodge in the forest). However, that could occur a presumption that defies the rational prepper guidelines.

Certain individuals say, "I can't envision a practical situation where I would have to bug out for more than a couple of days." You can choose to skip fabricating a packed-and-prepared bag if you'd like; however, you're choosing to be less ready. The general purpose is that you don't have the foggiest idea of what will occur, so why not have a constantly packed bag that can carry out twofold responsibilities in your home? The main time we believe it's levelheaded to avoid this progression is for older or impaired people who face steep difficulties outside the home.

There are endless circumstances where having this one bag, all set can make the difference between life or passing — or, if nothing else, the difference between going great or bunches of torment and lost cash. A few models:

Specialists request a departure, and you need to beat the tumult and gridlocks by leaving rapidly while others scramble to pack.

You need to get someplace quick (perhaps a relative is out of nowhere on their deathbed), and you lack the opportunity and willpower to pack a short-term bag.

You awaken around midnight to a house fire or quickly move toward a fierce blaze that torches your home soon after your escape.

Somebody is harmed outside your home, so you get your bag (which has clinical supplies) and run towards them.

The storm or cyclone you thought planned to miss you unexpectedly headed in a different direction, and now you're in a FEMA cover for a month.

A seismic tremor compels you outside, and you can't return to that frame of mind while they switch off the utility gas to stop the flames.

Common turmoil creates outside your home, and you need to get some distance.

A foe has gone after your area, maybe with a rocket or bio weapon.

A home gatecrasher or other abusive behavior at home implies you need to leave rapidly.

Your go-bag has what you need to make due, similar to water and a safe house, while additionally including things to recuperate, such as significant records for the homeowner's protection or pictures of friends and family.

Also, that is the precarious part: How would you assemble the most balanced supplement of stuff you need to get by and recuperate in one bag? How would you fabricate that bag that covers the most stretched-out scope of commonsense situations as could be expected?

More: Why you ought to utilize a focused on bag framework rather than bags in view of timelines

STAGE 3: BUG OUT BAGS FOR EACH GROWN-UP

All the more precisely: a bug-out bag for everybody around the house who can convey them. For instance, numerous families build different bags for youngsters once they hit 10-12 years of age, modifying the items on a case-by-case basis.

For instance, an essential 20-pound "go bag" ought to have:

- Individual First Aid Kit - Level 1
- 32 oz consumable water stored in a hard container
- Folding container/vessel
- Water channel
- Water purification tablets x 20-40
- Food that is prepared to eat
- Lighter x 2
- Kindling
- Headlamp
- Field knife
- Multitool
- Cordage x 50'
- Canvas
- Waterproof paper and pen
- Reports (physical and USB thumb drive)
- Cash
- Dense cleanser
- Tissue
- Nail trimmers
- Cap
- Socks
- Top base layer
- Pants
- Clothing
- Coat/outer shell
- Shemagh/handkerchief/gaiter

- Portable radio
- USB charging link and divider plug
- Li-Ion battery pack
- Respirator
- Project worker garbage sacks x 2
- Capacity bags (20L drybag and 5x gallon Ziplocs)
- More: Great bug-out bag backpacks

STAGE 4: GET HOME BAGS, EVERYDAY CARRY, AND VEHICLE SUPPLIES

What occurs if an emergency strikes while you're away from home?

You obviously can't stroll around with a weighty bag constantly, so the key is to keep the right sorts of supplies where they normally fit within your life design — the vast majority's day-to-day designs will generally be reliable and unsurprising, so utilize that for your potential benefit.

Model situations:

A severely draining and tanked understudy is staggering around a rear entryway alone on a chilly Friday night.

Your metro vehicle loses in the middle between stations.

You witness a severe auto crash while driving home in heavy traffic. It could take emergency administrations 10 to 15 minutes to show up.

You're cornered by two muggers while heading home from your companion's condo around evening.

A shooter assaults irregular people while you're in the shopping center.

A quake strikes while you're working. Your vehicle is in the parking structure, and you work in the city about 30 minutes from your rural home.

For many people in present-day cultures, that implies a blend of:

One Get Home Bag (GHB) in your vehicle trunk, work storage, office or any place else tends to be securely stored such that it's close to you for however much of a typical day as could be expected.

Regular convey (EDC) things you keep with the rest of your personal effects consistently, either on your body or in an everyday use pack, for example, a school backpack or tote.

Vehicle supplies. Even if you retain a GHB in your trunk, it's wise to keep extra stuff specifically for vehicle issues.

The Get Home Bag gets its name from the idea of "Poo just hit everyone out of nowhere, so I need to return home because that is my essential spot!"

In any case, a GHB likewise fills in as your possible cause of supplies if the idea of the emergency implies you can't (or shouldn't) attempt to return home. For an outrageous model, envision a bioweapon is delivered between your work and home, meaning you need to evict the other way. A more normal model is going through a night in your vehicle during a snowstorm.

So a GHB is like a BOB in numerous ways, just kept outside of the home. You ought to utilize and modify the bug-out bag agenda.

Average loadout differences between a GHB and BOB:

Vehicle trunks can get extremely hot, so stay away from foods and prescriptions that dissolve at 100-150 degrees.

Just fill water compartments ~85% of the method for considering freeze development in chilly environments.

In regions with stricter weapons regulations, what you can lawfully keep stored in your BOB at home probably won't be legitimate in a GHB/EDC outside the home.

Since most Americans drive all over, the vehicle trunk is the most well-known capacity spot. Specific individuals venture to cover their GHB close to their work or on the route between work and home.

If you don't drive or simply don't can store an entire backpack someplace, give your all to coordinate the main supplies (e.g., a water channel) into your day-to-day use packs or handbags.

Ordinary Carry agenda

Since EDC things are actually conveyed wherever you go, you're considerably more restricted by space and weight. More than 95% of EDC things you find in the wild are produced using all or part of this rundown:

- In Case of Emergency subtleties (e.g., a covered card of significant data kept in a wallet)
- Telephone (generally with downloaded maps and helpful applications)
- Li-Ion battery-powered battery pack
- Spotlight
- Folding knife
- Multitool
- Lighter
- Blooper pack (less injury situated than an IFAK)
- Respirator
- Paracord
- Weatherproof scratch pad and pen
- Self-protection weapons, pepper showers, and so forth.
- Secret money and Mastercards

These things can be spread around to make sense for you. For instance, certain individuals keep the telephone and lighter in their pocket, the electric lamp on their keychain, the multitool and CCW gun on their belt, the paracord as a wrist armband, and the clinical supplies, respirator, USB battery, notebook, pen, and ICE data in their bag/handbag.

We don't suggest utilizing unbeatable body defensive layer, backpacks, or comparative defensive stuff for EDC. The trepidation around dynamic shooters is exaggerated — you're bound to bite the dust from winter ice — and the stuff, although viable in a vacuum, simply isn't down to earth for ordinary use (yet).

Vehicles

If you have a vehicle, you should save important stuff close by for street-related crises. These things needn't bother with to be kept in a backpack since it's impossible for you'll have to convey them by walking over a distance.

Famous stuff kept in the vehicle:

- In Case of Emergency, data is kept in a glove box or control center
- Maps
- Window breaker and safety belt shaper device
- Mylar emergency cover 1-2x
- Appropriate cover or an additional coat
- Additional cap, shades, sunscreen
- Kick-off battery
- Jumper links
- Tow straps
- Street flares or blast signal
- Spare tire
- Tire wrench
- Jack
- Tire fix pack (plug openings rather than supplant the entire tire)
- Windshield scrubber
- Deicing windshield cleaner
- A little digging tool (i.e., "e-instrument" or settling-in device) or nursery scoop for recovering tires
- Kitty litter, sand, or another spreadable footing
- Footing sheets
- Error unit, IFAK, Rx drugs, additional glasses, etc.
- Fitting to transform a cigarette lighter into a USB charger
- Stored water as well as a water channel

STAGE 5: LEARN, PRACTICE, AND PLAN!

Having gear is a certain something, yet endurance specialists know that an extraordinary prep is a blend of stuff, abilities, arranging, and practice.

And that implies you are not ready if you get some stuff, toss it away, then, at that point, applaud yourself!

You would rather not depend on an item in an emergency that you've never utilized. Even if something appears to be straightforward now, your cerebrum can transform into a bowl of mush when confronted with disarray.

For instance: Think a vehicle window breaker could be straightforward?

Also, there are many bad "endurance" items that go to pieces in the field when you really want them most. On the other hand, perhaps that lifeboat food you purchased doesn't agree with your stomach, which you don't understand until managing looseness of the bowels at the most terrible time.

Whenever you have a portion of the essential stuff set up across your home and go-bags, now is the right time to begin mastering basic abilities.

Do this in lined up as you keep fabricating your supplies past the rudiments and tweaking your fiasco readiness plan.

Although you can track down unexpected yet invaluable treasures free of charge on YouTube, it's difficult to tell which ones are genuine and which ones are some irregular person letting you know exposed endurance exhortation passed down from his grandpas.

Step up your abilities with our internet-based endurance courses, for example, figuring out how to deal with health-related crises when you're all alone or how to find and purify water.

BOOK 6: THE MOST EFFECTIVE METHOD TO COOK SIMPLE AND DELICIOUS FOOD WITHOUT WASTING A LOT OF TIME IN PREPARATION

Cooking at home can be so much tomfoolery and genuinely fulfilling, yet sometimes it is greatly improved when others are included. You get the moment of gratification of hearing somebody let you know how great the food is, and you get a feeling of achievement when everybody is complete and blissful. When do you need to cook for yourself? It tends to be difficult — even for the people who love to cook.

With regards to cooking for one, what to zero in on is proficiency. How would you diminish the cooking time while planning astounding meals that aren't quesadillas and oat? The following are five viable tips that will help you excel at cooking for one.

PRE-SEGMENT YOUR PROTEINS

To prepare different meals, you will need to purchase a lot of protein (consider cuts of chicken, pork, fish, tofu, and hamburger). Make sure you don't gorge by utilizing a kitchen scale to partition your proteins. This will permit you to know precisely the number of meals you will have with your staple take while likewise preventing you from consuming such a large number of calories. If separating protein into single servings isn't your thing, ponder buying frozen pre-divided choices. Chicken bosom and cuts of seafood are exceptionally simple to track down pre-arranged along these lines and could likewise help set aside your cash instead of purchasing new.

UTILIZE A SIMMERING POT

A smaller than expected simmering pot considers clump concocting without taking a great deal of room. Awaken on Sunday, set your simmering pot up with a recipe for the week, and let it cook while you partake in the remainder of your day with companions. When you return on Sunday night, you will eat for the evening — and a couple of evenings afterward.

GO FOR FROZEN FOODS OR NON-PERISHABLES

One typical obstruction for singles regarding shopping for food and preparing new is the likelihood that the food will turn sour. One method for combatting food waste is to search for frozen choices. Very few people perceive that frozen produce is comparably solid, if not more, than new; its blaze frozen and keeps up with every one of the supplements.

We want frozen single-serving vegetables that you can simply toss in the microwave and be finished. They even come in different flavors! While frozen foods are an extraordinary choice for produce, canned foods are also perfect for beans, fish, and, surprisingly, chicken. They can be purchased in mass and utilized for simple meals on any night when you can't be tried to go shopping for food. Canned chicken, dark beans, and microwaved veggies — that is a finished feast!.

STORE YOUR MEALS IN DISCRETE CAPACITY HOLDERS

While feast preparing for the week on Sunday makes for a simple supper during the week, it can likewise be exhausting to have precisely the same thing consistently. If you love to have another feast every evening, we suggest making each piece of the dinner (protein, carb, veggies) and putting each in a different holder in the fridge. This will give you a chance to blend and match different parts. To make this a stride further, do whatever it takes not to add flavors or spices to the dishes. Add them while warming the foods up the evening of all things being equal. This will take into account some space for error every night with the kinds of flavors you might need to appreciate.

FREEZE ANY MEALS THAT YOU WILL NOT GET TO THAT WEEK

One more method for diminishing the need to call for takeout is to freeze a few meals for a stormy day. There will be times you cook and leave for the end of the week. Have a few holders helpful for extras that you can hold up! These meals will be prepared for you when you want them the most.

While it might be challenging to come by the inspiration to cook for yourself, know that you are continuously picking the better choice. The primary objective is to keep the recipes straightforward, use apparatuses for clump cooking, go frozen and durable whenever the situation allows and pay special attention to very interesting items that make for simple feast prep. We likewise suggest welcoming companions over once in some time — just to make sure your concocting abilities are to standard!

For each feast of the day, including make-and-take morning meals and snacks, this is a cheap food that wellbeing specialists would support.

1. PEACH COBBLER OATMEAL

Disregard seasoned oats packets and go natural with this oat suggestive of a shoemaker. New peaches, slashed walnuts, or your nut of decision, and cinnamon will fulfill your sweet tooth so well that you might wind up making it for dessert.

2. STRAIGHTFORWARD POACHED EGG AND AVOCADO TOAST

Avocado toast is trendy, yet adding a poached egg takes it to another level and finishes the trifecta of nourishment: protein, fats, and carbs. Parmesan cheddar and new spices sprinkled on top make it look and taste extravagant.

3. OATS BLUEBERRY YOGURT PANCAKES

A pile of homemade hotcakes doesn't take that long to make. These are high-protein and liberated from gluten, yet they taste astonishing and soft on account of bananas, oats, vanilla, and blueberries.

4. CHEDDAR-GARLIC GRITS WITH FRIED EGGS

A Southern work of art, messy corn meal doesn't need to be a finished fat and calorie bomb. Cook them in water as opposed to draining and discard the margarine. Keep the cheddar: Both tablespoons for each serving here keeps the dish gooey and rich and give just about 10% of your daily calcium.

Then add eggs for resilience, hacked chives for their marginally oniony flavor, and garlic, making all that taste better.

5. HOT QUINOA CEREAL

Impressive for all intents and purposes, quinoa gets some margin to cook. While specific individuals have said that it tends to be nuked, requiring over 10 minutes in many microwaves. In any case, quinoa pieces, which are like oats yet are a finished protein, can be prepared instantly.

Blend them in your preferred milk with dried berries, and afterward, top away with nuts, nut spread, seeds, and new natural products.

6. MIXED TOFU

When appropriately ready, tofu is everything except blah — and this variant gives as much protein as a fried egg. Throw the vegetarian staple with messy nourishing yeast, turmeric, cumin, and paprika (purchase smoked for even more character). Even egg sweethearts will appreciate it.

7. PUMPKIN PIE OATMEAL

This solid harvest time motivated oats gets its pie-like flavor from pumpkin puree, pumpkin pie zest, cinnamon, and vanilla. A sprinkling of dried cranberries adds normal pleasantness.

8. OPEN-FACED SANDWICHES WITH RICOTTA, ARUGULA, AND FRIED EGG

A morning meal sandwich can be far beyond crushed bacon, egg, and cheddar eaten in the driver's seat. Indeed, this one requires a fork and knife; however, it's worth the effort.

Toasted bread is finished off with fiery arugula, a decent wellspring of vitamin K, which helps your blood coagulation. Then add an egg, pungent ricotta — it has more protein than curds — Parmesan, and thyme. It's a sandwich like no other.

9. OMELET IN A MUG

Throw your number one breakfast meat (or skip it if you're vegan), salsa, eggs, and cheddar in a mug and zap it for one moment. Mix, and afterward, cook for one more 30 to 45 seconds.

Season to taste and finish off with more cheddar. Breakfast has never been simpler to make — or to tidy up.

10. BUTTERNUT SQUASH RAMEN BOWL WITH RICE NOODLES, TOFU, AND FRESH PEA SHOOTS

A heavenly supper for one, this noodle bowl has all kinds of your favorite speedy cook noodle cups yet none of the yucky added substances. Rice noodles give the main part of this accommodating vegan bowl, which utilizations boxed butternut squash soup as a base for quick cooking.

Pea shoots taste like peas and are plentiful in nutrients An and C and folic corrosive. If you can't find them, you can utilize spinach.

11. MEDITERRANEAN PANZANELLA

Instead of the top of a plate of mixed greens with bagged croutons, prepare this Tuscan form with toasted pita bread.

There are the typical great alone-yet better-together suspects expected in something many refer to as "Mediterranean": tomatoes, cucumbers, feta, and olives. The olives are essential since the fats in them help your body retain the supplements in the veggies.

12. CRUNCHY ASIAN RAMEN NOODLE SALAD

This beautiful, crunchy salad is exactly what is needed when mixed greens-based assortments are exhausting you.

Crunchy coleslaw blend and dried ramen noodles (trade-in crunchy rice noodles for a less-handled choice) are thrown with avocado for sound fat, edamame for protein, and mango for vision-safeguarding beta-carotene.

13. SPEEDY AND EASY CHICKEN BURRITO

Extra chicken tracks down another home in this fast burrito. Blend it with avocado and cheddar before enveloping it with a tortilla and cooking it. We'd make it one stride further and add a few peppers, onions, and perhaps greens to the filling. Reward: Make a couple without a moment's delay and freeze the additional items for an even quicker lunch sometime later.

14. SALMON AND HERBED BEAN SALAD

Exhausted with fish salad? Attempt canned salmon blended in with rich cannellini beans, veggies, and new spices for a really simple dinner that is, however, delectable all alone as it could be in a pita or with entire grain wafers.

15. RICH BUFFALO CHICKEN AND BLACK BEAN QUESADILLAS

If you generally go after the wings on game day, this is the lunch quesadilla. It's fiery, smooth, and stacked with flavor. Dark beans knock up the fiber and protein, and green onions add some additional punch. Go ahead and downsize on the sou.

HOW TO HUNT AND FISH (AND MAKE ANIMAL TRAPS)

If you end up running out of food in the wild, you can remain alive on a natural product, vegetables, and roots you could find, however not for a really long time. These foods are plentiful in minor elements and nutrients; however, they don't give the energy you want that comes from protein and fat. To make due in the wild, meat is important to meet your everyday healthful necessities.

Hunting is an effective method for supporting your endurance diet, yet if you make no kills, you may be sitting around idly and inviting starvation. Fishing and trapping little game can be an appealing other option.

Getting food this way enjoys many benefits. If set at the ideal places, catches and traps can productively give food to you and your buddies while requiring negligible exertion.

Traps don't have to rest, nor do they need you to look after them. Setting a few up at a time resembles utilizing a few trackers for nothing, every minute of every day.

DON'T BE SQUEAMISH

While trapping little creatures for food, you can't stand to be demanding. Be ready to trap and eat animals you've never eaten. Birds, reptiles, rodents, fish, eels, worms, and certain bugs. Essentially anything that creeps, swims, flies or crawls that has non-harmful meat ought to be on the menu.

The watchword here is energy: the typical grown-up American male necessities between 2,400 to 3,000 calories each day as indicated by the USDA. However long your catch is palatable and nontoxic, everyday food overshadows individual preferences and tastes.

THE TOOLS YOU'LL NEED

To make the traps, you'll need a knife, or if nothing else, whatever can cut or cut. Twine, rope, string, or metal wire can execute excellent cutting. If you don't have a rope, the foundations of little trees like tidy are great substitutes.

GET YOUR WORK DONE

Before you make and put out the snares, first, you need to figure out what kind of game is accessible to you. Then, study what sort of tracks they leave, what kind of living space they have, what time of day they're dynamic, and what kind of food they eat.

Knowing what food they eat is significant since you'll need to bait your traps. The following are a couple of tips for traps you can set up.

CATCHES

Catches comprise tough material designed into a noose, similar to twine, wire, or slim rope, but outside the game's nook or following right after it. The noose should be large enough for the creature's head to go through, and, contingent upon the development, the catch might be set off to "whip" the animal brutally and break its neck or choke it as it battles to break free.

To make a viable catch, you should know how to make a legitimate bunch and a scored trigger if you have any desire to utilize one. You can build your odds by doing it the best way with a catch by using bait.

DEADFALLS

Deadfalls are traps that utilize powerful things, like huge shakes or logs, to smash a creature. An exemplary model is the Figure-Four Deadfall. The name comes from the indented sticks that structure the number "4".

The level stick upholds the stone or log while holding the bait, subsequently going about as a weighted trigger.

BIRD TRAPS

While Deadfalls can get birds, one sort of trap is specifically made for the winged game: the Pine Pitch Bird Cup. Note that you ought to involve this in an endurance circumstance, as it is viewed as an unlawful and brutal strategy for trapping.

For this trip, all you want is a vacant espresso or dixie cup, some bait (like bird seed), and sticky pine sap or pitch. The first local variant purposes a little cone of Birch tree rind sewed to frame a cone.

Within is covered with sticky pine sap or pitch blended in with the bait. When a bird is drawn in by the bait, its plumes stall out in the pitch, holding it fixed until the trapper can gather it.

PIT TRAPS

The size of creatures this trap can get is restricted simply by how enormous you make it. The main downsides to this trap are that it takes a ton of energy to art, and it should be put near a game path.

Notwithstanding these disadvantages, it's a decent trap to use because of its basic development and effectiveness. To start with, find a path where creatures as often as possible pass, as shown by tracks, droppings, or upset vegetation. Dig a pit profound and wide enough to trap and hold the creature you need.

Place sharp sticks at the base, then, at that point, make a barbecue of sticks and branches to cover the pit. Conceal the barbecue with leaves and grass.

How a pit trap ought to seem to be.

FISH TRAPS

If you're near a waterway or stream, a fish trap is a reliable approach to enhancing your eating regimen with nutritious seafood. You can make a straightforward and powerful pool

119

or shore fish trap by setting up rocks and a few sticks to a pipe and afterward "close-in" fish near the shore.

Make sure you construct the entry of your trap inverse to the current to prevent the fish from leaving when they enter your trap.

If you're near the ocean, the salt marsh trap can help you exploit the tide's recurring pattern. Make a sickle-formed mass of rocks during low tide, with the "tips" of the bow pointing away from the waterway.

The divider ought to be constructed so that it expands outward and into the water. The divider should be sufficiently high to stand out at low tide, trapping fish when the tide goes out.

The basket trap can work regardless of the current and with the additional temptation of bait. It comprises adaptable branches attached to plants or more slender branches in a cone or channel shape. The basket trap is tied safely to shore or overloaded with rocks inside.

The entry of the basket is fixed with an internal pointing cone, tricking the fish into figuring they can't get out. The upside of these traps is the incredible outcomes you can get from generally little exertion.

The basket trap is a piece difficult to make, yet when it works, it's entirely supportable and can be utilized repeatedly. You can begin with a pine cone to bait your most memorable fish, then, at that point, use its guts to bait the following fish, whose guts bait the following, etc.

As the basket is woven vertical, the in the middle between posts increments considering the utilization of the bigger and frequently less adaptable grape plants. Bigger plants are more inclined to holes. Be that as it may, they can radically accelerate the basket-production process with scrupulousness.

NOTES ON TRAPS

Like land, the way to viable traps is area. Put out snares in regions where you can see proof of game "traffic."

Great spots to put traps incorporate regions near water sources.

Your fragrance can put off creatures from taking the bait. Veil your fragrance by blowing smoke on the trap or scouring mud, soil, or leaves on your hands when you handle the trap.

Try not to stick around and hold on to check whether your traps find anything. Creatures might find your trail and remain away. Each time you put out a snare, leave the region.

Take a look at your traps at regular intervals for an effective catch. This is a sensible range of time to get any catch before it spoils or different hunters take them.

While not setting or checking your traps, utilize the time all the more productively by scrounging, cover building, or other endurance fundamental assignments.

HUNTING GIGS

While trusting that your traps will spring, spend most of your time hunting with an ad-libbed pronged lance or "gig." This is a crude instrument for getting fish.

To make a gig, all you want is a sharp knife, a sensibly straight, skewer length stick, cordage, and a few twigs. To begin with, cut a "+" into one finish of the stick to isolate it into four equivalent quarters. Chop about five creeps down the shaft of the stick, delicately parting it open, so it structures four "prongs."

Then, get two twigs, embedding consistently between the prongs and opposite the shaft and one another, by delicately tapping one finish of the twig while squeezing the opposite end with your thumb. This will isolate the prongs, setting out four open doors to skewer your prey. The twigs ought to be situated about three crawls from the end of the shaft.

Hone every one of the four prongs to a point. Fortify the prongs by cautiously turning them over a pit fire. Do this for about 10-15 minutes, ensuring that the gig doesn't burst into flames.

When the prongs have adequately evaporated and hardened, secure both little stakes with cordage, and wrap the gig with cordage for about 1 inch on both sides of the twigs to prevent it from parting open upon influence. Now you have a hunting gig to stick fish or any little creature you go over.

HOW TO COOK FOOD EVEN IF THERE IS NO ELECTRICITY OR RUNNING WATER

As a general public, we have become familiar with our cutting-edge comforts. Besides cooking on a stovetop or broiler, we can pop a dish in the microwave and have it prepared in only seconds! So when we wind up in a position where we don't approach these comforts, things can get extreme.

Whether you are out on an end of the week setting up a camp excursion, abandoned in the forest, or in other desperate conditions, knowing how to cook without modern machines and devices is essential. The following are eight elective ways you can cook without power:

SUN ORIENTED COOKER

What better method for cooking in nature than using the power of the sun? Most sunlight-based fueled cookers are lightweight and foldable, making them wonderful to welcome on setting up camp excursions or stored for crises. True to form, splendid skies and hotter temperatures help the sunlight-based cooker work at max execution. Particularly if you are exploring nature or where an open fire isn't a choice, sun-based cookers are an extraordinary elective strategy for preparing a warm dinner. Shockingly enough, food temperature can reach 225°F with this technique!

Notwithstanding the sun-based cooker displayed underneath, consider growing your emergency and home cooking with the utilization of sun-oriented fueled gadgets. Sunlight-based power gives excellent off-lattice and outdoor power answers for any circumstance. Not exclusively is it eco-accommodating, sun-oriented power packs and boards, similar to those from GoalZero, can be charged and utilized just when required.

ROCKET STOVES

Rocket stoves are a little effective and especially helpful when you are coming up with short ablaze beginning supplies, as very little fuel is required. A rocket stove utilizes a little ignition chamber to consume limited quantities of wood. An upward stack is joined to the chamber - guiding intensity directly to the top surface. This arrangement considers almost complete ignition before arriving at the cooking surface. Those in outrageous conditions could construct a makeshift rocket stove out of metal jars if vital.

OPEN FIRE

There isn't anything cruder than cooking over an open fire. If the supplies are accessible and open flames are permitted, this strategy might be the most useful. Never be without fire beginning apparatuses and supplies, for example, matches, kindling, stone, or dry wood. Likewise, forever know about your environmental factors and make a blockade that prevents your fire from spreading. Open flames consider a few cooking choices: skillets and dishes can be painstakingly positioned in the fire, laid on hot coals, or securely upon barbecue tops over the fire. If the cooking gear is restricted or excessively weighty for your pack, food can be shrouded in aluminum foil and painstakingly situated on or close to the hot coals.

COLLAPSING STEEL STOVE

Collapsing steel stoves measure just six creeps by 6 inches - yet they are as yet sufficiently able to hold an enormous pot and effectively carry water to bubble in under thirty minutes. The stove overlays level making it simple to take in a hurry. These little and proficient stoves work on canned fuel, so stock up with a good inventory, and you'll be prepared to prepare a warm feast immediately.

KELLY KETTLE

During emergency circumstances or when power is lost, the capacity to bubble water is critical. A Kelly Kettle makes it simple to do precisely that, bubble water or even intensity a soup or stew. You start by building a fire in the base and setting the pot on top. Kelly Kettle's work with any normal fuel and keep up with their intensity with extra fuel sources (twigs, leaves, paper, and so on) being dropped down the stack. The pot's capacity to bubble water rapidly might be the difference between remaining hydrated or drinking sullied ailment-causing water.

CONVENIENT BUTANE STOVES

Convenient butane stoves might be the nearest to a conventional cooking technique, matching the strength of a home gas or electric stovetop. Because these little, movable stoves run on butane canisters, they are a genuinely modest method for cooking in the wild and can be stored for emergency use. With a few choices to look over, picking the right one for your necessities might befuddle. For people who prefer a solid yet lightweight stove, the Mountain Series from Camp Chef will fulfill your requirements. If a calm stove with simple capacity is significant, consider the Multi-Fuel Cooktop.

SPRING OF GUSHING LAVA STOVES

If weak cooking and flexibility are significant, think about a Volcano Stove. Spring of gushing lava Stove is maybe the simplest to pack and store as the stove the folding and creases down to 5 inches! Also, Volcano Stoves permit you to cook with propane, charcoal, or wood - with adaptability to barbecue, heat, smoke, sear, or grill your supper.

MOTOR

To wrap things up, when you have depleted any remaining choices, cooking with your car engine might be achievable. Turn on and run the vehicle inactive to warm the engine; when the engine has arrived at a significant temperature, switch off the motor. Then, cautiously put your skillet or thwarted food on the hot engine. Nonetheless, before utilizing this cooking procedure, generally check your gas level; the last thing you believe you should do is run entirely out of juice and leave yourself abandoned.

Essentially all emergency circumstances can be moderated with legitimate preparation and planning. Being outfitted with both knowledge and the appropriate instruments is pivotal for progress, no matter your situation.

BOOK 7: INTRODUCTION TO HOME MEDICAL

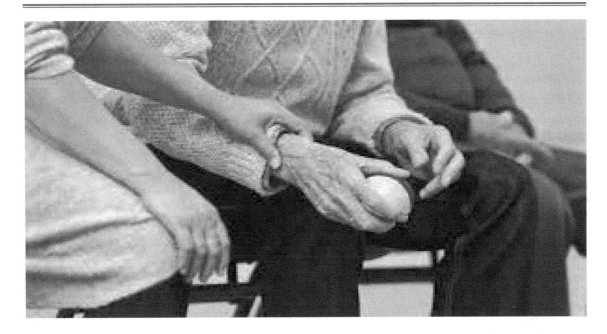

The idea of the "home medical" has advanced starting from the primary presentation of the American Academy of Pediatrics in 1967. At that point, it was imagined as a focal hotspot for all the medical data about a kid, particularly those with unique necessities. Endeavors by Calvin C.J. Sia, MD, a pediatrician, in the quest for new ways to deal with further develop youth improvement in Hawaii during the 1980s laid the basis for an Academy strategy proclamation in 1992 that characterized a medical home to a great extent how Sia imagined it: a methodology for conveying the family-focused, exhaustive, persistent, and facilitated care that all babies and youngsters merit. In 2002, the association extended and operationalized the definition.

In 2002, seven U.S. public family medicine associations made the Eventual fate of Family Medicine undertaking to "change and recharge the specialty of family medicine." Among the proposals of the venture was that each American ought to have an "individual medical home" through which they could get intense, persistent, and preventive health administrations. These administrations should be "open, responsible, far-reaching, coordinated, patient-focused, safe, scientifically legitimate, and fulfilling to both patients and their doctors."

A survey of this declaration, distributed later that year, discovered that medical homes are "related with better health,... with lower in general expenses of care and with decreases in health."

By 2005, the American School of Doctors had fostered a "high-level medical home" model. This model included using proof-based medicine, clinical choice help instruments, the Persistent Care Model, medical care plans, "upgraded and advantageous" admittance to care, quantitative marks of value, health data innovation, and input on execution. Installment change was wisely perceived as vital to the performance of the model.

WHAT IS MEDICINE

Medicine is regularly characterized as a substance or readiness that can treat or forestall illness. By and large, most medicines are produced using regular items. Propels over the most recent two centuries have prompted the presentation of artificial substance medicines, biologics, and quality treatments. Furthermore, innovations, such as tissue designing, which utilizes living cells to fix tissues or organs, and nanomedicine, which uses minuscule 'nanoparticles in various healthcare settings, have expanded the choices accessible.

Medicine is the science and practice of focusing on a patient, dealing with the finding, guess, counteraction, treatment, mitigation of their physical issue or sickness, and advancing their health. Medicine envelops an assortment of healthcare rehearses developed to keep up with and reestablish health by counteracting and treating illness. Contemporary medicine applies biomedical sciences, biomedical exploration, hereditary qualities, and medical innovation to analyze, treat, and forestall injury and infection, regularly through drugs or medical procedures, yet in addition through treatments as different as psychotherapy, outer braces and footing, medical gadgets, biologics, and ionizing radiation, among others.

Medicine has been polished since ancient times, during the more significant part of which was a craft (an area of expertise and information) now and again having associations with nearby culture's strict and philosophical convictions. For instance, a medicine man would apply spices and express petitions for recuperating, or an old savant and doctor would use blood draining as indicated by the hypotheses of humorism. In hundreds of years since the approach of current science, most medicine has turned into a mix of craftsmanship and science (both fundamental and applied, under the umbrella of medical science). While the sewing procedure for stitches is craft educated through training, the information on what occurs at the cell and sub-atomic level in the tissues being sewed emerges through science.

Prescientific types of medicine are presently known as traditional medicine or socialized medicine, which remains generally utilized without any scientific medicine, and are accordingly called elective medicine. Elective medicines beyond scientific medicine having well-being and adequacy concerns are named deception.

Medicines are synthetic substances or mixtures used to fix, stop, or forestall sickness, ease side effects, or help conclude ailments. Propels in medicines have empowered specialists to cure numerous illnesses and save lives.

Medicine has been polished since ancient times, during a large portion of which it was a craft (an area of expertise and information) regularly having associations with the strict and philosophical convictions of neighborhood culture. For instance, a medicine man would apply spices and express petitions for mending, or an old scholar and doctor would use phlebotomy as per the speculations of humorism. In late hundreds of years, since the appearance of present-day science, most medicine has turned into a blend of craft and science (both essential and applied, under the umbrella of medical science). While sewing strategy for stitches is a scholarly craft through training, the information on what occurs at the cell and sub-atomic level in the tissues being sewed emerges through science.

Prescientific types of medicine are currently known as conventional medicine or socialized medicine, which remains usually utilized without a trace of scientific medicine, and are called elective medicine. Elective medicines beyond scientific medicine having well-being and adequacy concerns are named deception.

Medical accessibility and clinical practice shifts worldwide because of provincial contrasts in culture and innovation. Current scientific medicine is profoundly evolved in the

Western world. At the same time, in emerging nations, for example, portions of Africa or Asia, the populace might depend vigorously on traditional medicine with restricted proof and adequacy and no necessary conventional preparation for experts.

In the created world, proof-based medicine isn't generally utilized in that frame of mind; for instance, a 2007 overview of writing surveys saw that around 49% of the mediations needed adequate proof to help either advantage or damage.

Nowadays, drugs come from various sources. Some are extracted from substances tracked down in nature, and, surprisingly, many are disengaged from plants today.

A few medicines are made in labs by combining various synthetic substances. Others, similar to penicillin, are side effects of living beings like an organism. Furthermore, a couple is even organically designed by embedding qualities into microbes that make them produce the ideal substance.

When we contemplate taking medicines, we often consider pills.

In present-day clinical practice, doctors and doctor colleagues survey patients to analyze, prognosis, treat, and forestall sickness utilizing a clinical judgment. The specialist-patient relationship ordinarily starts a connection with an assessment of the patient's medical history and medical record, trailed by a medical meeting and an actual evaluation. Fundamental analytic medical gadgets (such as stethoscopes and tongue depressors) are regularly utilized. After assessment for signs and meeting for side effects, the specialist might arrange medical tests (for example, blood tests), take a biopsy, or endorse drug drugs or different treatments. Differential finding strategies help to preclude conditions in light of the data given. During the experience, appropriately advising the patient regarding all practical realities is a significant piece of the relationship and the advancement of trust. The medical expertise is then reported in the medical record, an authoritative record in numerous jurisdictions. However, subsequent meet-ups might be more limited follow a similar general system, and experts follow a comparative cycle. The conclusion and treatment might require a couple of moments or half a month, depending on the intricacy of the issue.

VARIOUS KINDS OF MEDICINES

Medicines act in an assortment of ways. Some can fix an ailment by killing or ending the spread of attacking microbes, like bacteria and infections. Others are utilized to regard malignant growth by killing cells as they partition or keeping them from duplicating. A few medications supplant missing substances or low right degrees of regular body synthetics like a few chemicals or nutrients. Medicines might influence portions of the sensory system that control a body cycle.

Almost everybody has taken an anti-infection. This kind of medication battles bacterial diseases. Your primary care physician might endorse an anti-toxin for strep throat or ear disease. Anti-toxins work either by killing bacteria or ending their augmentation with the goal that the body's safe framework can fend off the contamination.

Once in a while, a piece of the body can't make a sufficient compound. That can likewise make you debilitated. Somebody with insulin-subordinate diabetes, for example, has a pancreas that can't create enough insulin (a chemical that manages glucose in the body). Specific individuals have a low creation of thyroid chemicals, which helps control how the body utilizes energy. For each situation, specialists can recommend medicines to supplant the missing chemical.

A few medicines treat side effects yet can't fix the sickness that causes the side effects. (A side effect is anything you feel while wiped out, like a hack or illness.) So taking a tablet might relieve an irritated throat, yet it won't kill that terrible strep bacteria.

A few medicines ease torment. Your PCP could advise you to take ibuprofen or acetaminophen if you pull a muscle. These pain killers, or analgesics, don't dispose of the wellspring of the aggravation; your strength will, in any case, be pulled. They block the pathways that communicate torment signals from the harmed or disturbed body part to the mind (all in all, they influence how the cerebrum peruses the aggravation signal) so you don't hurt as much while your body recuperates.

HOME MEDICAL

Home medical is best portrayed as a model or reasoning of essential care that shows restraint-focused, exhaustive, group-based, composed, open, and zeroed in on quality and well-being. It has turned into a generally acknowledged model for how essential care ought to be coordinated and conveyed all through the health care framework and is a way of thinking of health care conveyance that supports suppliers and care groups to meet patients where they are, from the easiest to the most intricate circumstances. It is where patients are treated with deference, respect, and sympathy and empowered with solid and entrusting associations with suppliers and staff. Most importantly, the medical home is certainly not the last objective. All things being equal, it is a model for accomplishing essential care greatness so that care is gotten ideally located, with impeccable timing, and in the way that best suits a patient's requirements.

FEATURES OF THE HOME MEDICAL

⌉ Patient-focused: An organization among practitioners, patients, and their families guarantees that choices regard patients' needs, requirements, and inclinations and that patients have the training and backing they need to decide and take part in their care.

⌉ Far-reaching: A group of care suppliers is entirely responsible for a patient's physical and psychological well-being care needs, including counteraction and health, intense care, and constant care.

⌉ Composed: Care is coordinated across all components of the more extensive health care framework, including specialty care, emergency clinics, home health care, community administrations, and support.

⌉ Available: Patients can get to administrations with more limited holding up times, "late night" care, every minute of electronic or phone access, and areas of strength for and through health IT advancements.

⌉ Focused on quality and security: Clinicians and staff upgrade quality improvement to guarantee that patients and families arrive at informed conclusions about their health,

⌉ Persistent: a similar essential care clinician cares for the kid from the outset through youthful adulthood, giving Help and backing to change to grown-up care.

⌉ Socially Viable: The family and youngster's way of life, language, convictions, and customs are perceived, esteemed, and regarded

HERBAL/NATURAL REMEDIES

Herbal remedies are plants utilized like a medication. Individuals use herbal remedies to help forestall or fix sickness. They use them to get alleviation from side effects, support energy, unwind, or get in shape.

Herbal remedies/cures are substances that come from plants. They come in different designs, for instance, compartments, teas, liquid drops, or skin creams. You can get them at well-being food shops, general stores, drug stores, and herbal practitioners.

Some might be referred to as 'supplements.' Others might be referred to as 'medicines,' implying they expect to treat, fix or forestall an analyzed health issue.

Herbal medicines are those with dynamic fixings produced using plant parts, like leaves, roots, or blossoms. Yet, being "regular" doesn't be guaranteed to mean they're alright for you to take.

Like regular medicines, herbal medicines will affect the body and be unsafe if they are not utilized accurately.

They ought to, in this manner, be utilized with similar care and regard as regular medicines.

If you're counseling your primary care physician or drug specialist about health matters or going through a medical procedure, consistently inform them concerning any herbal medicines you're taking.

HOW TO CREATE A MEDICINE CABINET AT HOME USING NATURAL REMEDIES

Whether you are battling irritated eyes or a blocked chest, there are spices in your nursery that individuals have depended on for a long time. When attempting to utilize every regular fixing, these should be the primary things you keep in your comprehensive medication bureau.

HOME REMEDIES FOR BODY ACHES & PAIN

NATURAL PAIN-RELIEF BALM

This salve mitigates sore muscles with the sorcery of turmeric and cayenne pepper. It feels warm when you apply it to your skin. Turmeric facilitates irritation in your body while the cayenne pepper warms the tissues and battles the aggravation you feel. I use it after I get a sensitive back from planting.

TUB TEA

An Epsom salt douse is an extraordinary method for relieving the day's hurts away. Adding spices and different botanicals can likewise be skin mitigating; however, tidying up after the bath is not excessively much tomfoolery. Make tub teas for a shower splash that is mending and requires no tidy-up a while later.

HERBAL FOOT SOAK

Now and again, you feel sickly. When this occurs, adding a couple of scoops of this to a bowl of warm water and dousing your feet assists you with feeling significantly improved. The steam from these recuperating foot douses additionally helps with a clog. Spoil yourself with this homemade foot douse produced using spices from your nursery.

PAMPERING PEPPERMINT FOR FEET

Cooling peppermint is made for sore feet. Shedding sugar and dried spices will scour away rough skin, coconut oil will relax breaks, and mitigating peppermint medicinal balm has a cooling, torment-easing impact.

ROLL-ON HEADACHE RELIEF

When I first feel cerebral pain coming on, I utilize a roller bottle with natural oils to get it before it gets energy. Typically this is all I need to boot the cerebral pain out. Roller bottle remedies are extraordinary to keep close by in the medication bureau.

HOME REMEDIES FOR TOPICAL SKIN RELIEF

FIRST AID SALVE FROM CALENDULA

I utilize this salve instead of a petrol-based germicide cream. I use my all-regular calendula salve on minor injuries and cuts. Using on pets and children is gentle and thoroughly protected. Besides, it smells superb!

TOPICAL ANTIFUNGAL TREATMENT

This homemade tea tree oil antifungal treatment stick assists with calming red spots and rashes in a delicate yet direct manner. It's bundled in a helpful cylinder so you can treat the sore, difficult spots rapidly.

DRAWING SALVE RECIPE FOR BUG BITES, BLISTERS, SPLINTERS

A drawing salve combines oils and herbal fixings that work to remove poisons from your skin. It can be utilized on mosquito chomps, wasp or honey bee stings, rankles, bubbles, bites, and minor contaminations.

DANDELION SALVE

Try not to kill the dandelions in your yard - it could be utilized to make an aggravation-easing salve. These yellow weeds have torment-reducing and mitigating properties. Utilize this salve on throbbing muscles and different afflictions you have.

COLD SORES AND LITTLE RED SPOTS

Lemon balm's antiviral properties make it a well-known spice for treating cold sores, chicken pox, bug nibbles, and other minimal red spots. This recipe for lemon balm lip balm not just has a brilliant and happy lemon scent; however, it likewise is an extraordinary method for forestalling and treating cold sores.

PROTECTING CUTICLES

This alleviating fingernail skin balm is loaded with a natural mix that will patch those breaks and make hands delicate in the future. It's vital to treat dry hands while doing a ton of hand washing.

HAND & BODY LOTION

Salve might be a wonder item decision instead of a homegrown cure. Yet, this one is produced using skin-calming botanical water and supporting oils that assist in fixing and safeguarding dry skin. Keeping skin delicate assists with keeping it sound, as I'm never without this recipe.

NATURAL SKIN SOOTHER

Use quieting witch hazel to alleviate razor consumption and rashes and cool down aggravation. It's produced using the parts of the witch hazel tree and can likewise be utilized as a face toner.

WHAT MEDICINE SHOULD YOU HAVE WITH YOU JUST IN CASE SOMETHING HAPPENS

ALLERGY MEDICATION

Contingent upon the season and where you reside, supplied medicine cupboards should contain eye drops and allergy medicines. Furthermore, Holder suggests keeping both a "sleepy" allergy med (for use before bed) and a non-tired allergy medicine (for use during the day) close by.

ANTI-BACTERIAL CREAM OR OINTMENT

Against bacterial creams and salves are utilized to treat or forestall minor skin diseases resulting from little pieces, scraped spots, or bug nibbles. "There is a contrast between a cream and salve, so you need to pick which turns out best for your necessities," said Holder. "Creams are water dissolvable, and clients should apply them after the injury is washed with a cleaning agent and water. Holder prescribes impacted persons to apply the counter bacterial cream when they stay inside where sweat is more uncertain. Balms are oil-based and can be utilized when the individual may be presented to water."

DECONGESTANT

Decongestants commonly found behind the drug store counter frequently have pseudoephedrine, which is used to create methamphetamine or meth. Consequently, Holder often suggests decongestants found on the standard racks of the drug store; however, decongestants found behind the counter function admirably.

PAIN KILLER

While picking a pain killer for your medicine bureau, assess your family's requirements. However, some agony medication should be required regularly," said Holder. "Consider which pain killers end up being savage for your necessities, and pick no less than one to have close by. If you have kids in your family, make certain to stock youngsters' pain killers."

ANTI-DIARRHEAL

"Especially families have small kids, or even older individuals, medicine cupboards ought to have an enemy of diarrheal," Holder said. This medication works by dialing back stomach development, which diminishes how much effects and makes the stool less watery.

CALAMINE LOTION

Calamine salve is an extraordinarily effective help for minor skin disturbances like a bug chomp or little consumption. The salve can reduce sensations of irritation, and, on account of a bug nibble, Holder said matching the calamine moisturizer with an allergy med is brilliant too.

ACTUATED CHARCOAL

Particularly with small kids, guardians ought to have something to actuate spewing on account of an unintentionally ingested poison. "Actuated charcoal is better at watching all items in the stomach than syrup of ipecac," added Holder. "Be that as it may, when you thought somebody gulped a toxic substance or ingested too many medications, whether over-the-counter or remedy, nothing can fill in for proficient assistance. If expert assistance isn't promptly accessible, then, at that point, you ought to direct actuated

135

charcoal, meanwhile, unafraid of significant mischief to the patient. The most well-known aftereffects are dark stools, dark tongue, and regurgitating or losing bowels. Initiated charcoal might cause stoppage assuming you control excessively, so clients should adhere to the measurement rules.

GLUE WRAPS

On account of a cut or scraped spot, glue wraps are critical to have close by because they offer an actual boundary of security for any painful injury. Specific individuals also like to have 2×2 glue cloth cushions with tape for the more significant cuts or scraped spots.

NASAL SUCTION TOOL BULB

Nasal suction tool bulbs help get bodily fluid out of little noses for families with small kids. It would help if you came to perfect and kept the nasal suction tool bulbs dry to forestall microbes moving to start with the one relative and then onto the next screen.

THERMOMETER

Holder says any thermometer will do; however, he suggests staying away from the mercury glass thermometers. Standard advanced thermometers are genuinely economical and give exact temperature readings.

TWEEZERS

Tweezers are valuable for eliminating splinters, yet did you realize they are likewise helpful for removing ticks? The best practice is to keep a couple of tweezers with sharp finishes close.

CAPACITY AND REMOVAL TIPS

When you have these provisions collected, keep them in a single spot — however, away from the washroom. "Do not keep your medicine bureau in the restroom. Dampness can affect, and now and again can inactivate medication," Holder said.

HOW TO KNOW THE MEDICINE ONE BRINGS WILL SOLVE ANY HEALTH PROBLEM

Medication plays a significant part in overseeing sickness, yet it can also be very hurtful when taken erroneously. It's sufficiently not to realize that you take a blue case and a yellow tablet two times per day. You need to know the names of your remedies and comprehend the significant insights concerning how they work. For instance, a few medicines might communicate gravely with specific food sources, different medications, or even food supplements and can make you extremely sick. Find an opportunity to find out about the treatment recommended for you. Your doctor or your drug specialist can assist with responding to these inquiries — feel free!

• What is the name of the medicine?

• For what reason do I have to take it?

• When and how might I take it? With water? With food? While starving?

• They are sum would it be wise for me to take? How would it be a good idea for me to respond if I missed a portion?

• What the medication could bring about secondary effects? Which ones would it be fitting for me to call the specialist about?

• Are there any food varieties or medicines I should avoid while taking this medicine?

• Will this medication change how my different medicines work?

As well as asking your doctor or drug specialist to assist you with understanding your medicines, find these ways to guarantee your security additionally.

• Continuously fill your remedies at a similar drug store. Like that, your medical history is on a document in one spot.

• Get a reality sheet about your medication from your drug specialist.

• Keep a rundown in your wallet or handbag of the relative multitude of solutions and over-the-counter medicines you take. Make sure to incorporate nutrients, well-being enhancements, and homegrown cures. Update the rundown at whatever point there are changes in your daily schedule. Note the name of everything, the measurement, why, and when you need to take it.

• Let your doctor and drug specialist know if you have any ailments or sensitivity to any medication or food, or on the other hand, if you are pregnant or breastfeeding.

BEST ACTION TO TAKE IF ONE OF YOUR FAMILY MEMBERS IS INJURED

Because of their unpredictable nature, emergency circumstances are frequently turbulent. Individuals respond to various events in various ways. It is highly expected for a person to lose self-control during an emergency and fail to remember the right moves to make. Even though it is fundamental to have a definite emergency plan, one ought to likewise have an exceptionally essential idea of what to do in case of an emergency.

By making a "First Things To Make" list, whether at home or in everyday life, you can be sure that everybody in question will know how to deal with themselves in an emergency. Every emergency circumstance is unique, yet there are essential rules that can help you through any episode that could happen. The accompanying rundown of the main activities in any emergency contains general tips that could fit most circumstances.

FIRST THINGS IN ANY EMERGENCY

• Remain composed. It will permit you to think obviously and utilize sound judgment.

• Access the situation for risk. Conclude whether it is more secure to empty or asylum set up.

• When securely emptied or sheltered set up, call for Help utilizing 911 and make sense of what you are familiar with the circumstance.

• Give medical aid to any injured individuals. Move any individuals who are injured away from additional risk.

• Get as much data about the emergency as reasonably expected without seriously endangering yourself. Give the data to emergency responders when they show up on the scene.

BOOK 8: INTRODUCTION TO FIRST AIDS

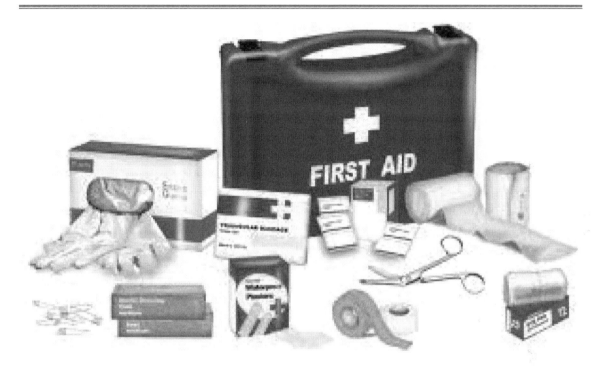

Skills of what is currently known as first aid have been recorded for ages, exceptionally comparable to fighting, where the care of horrible medical cases is expected in incredibly huge numbers. There are various references to first aid performed inside the Roman armed force, with an arrangement of first aid upheld by specialists, field ambulances, and clinics. Roman armies played the particular part of capsaicin, who was answerable for first aid like gauzing and are the precursors of the cutting edge battle doctor.

Further models happen through history, still for the most part connected with a fight, with models like the Knights Hospitaller in the eleventh-century Promotion, giving care to pioneers and knights in the Blessed Land.

The essential objective of first aid is to keep demise or genuine injury from deteriorating. The critical points of first aid can be summed up with the abbreviation of 'the three Ps.'

• Safeguard life: The abrogating point of all medical care that incorporates first aid is to save lives and limit the danger of death. First aid done accurately ought to assist with lessening the patient's degree of agony and quieting them down during the assessment and treatment process.

• Forestall further mischief: Counteraction of additional damage incorporates tending to both outside factors, for example, creating some distance from any reason for hurt, and applying first aid methods to forestall deteriorating conditions, for example, using strain to stop a drain from becoming perilous.

• Advance recuperation: First aid likewise includes attempting to begin the recuperation cycle from the disease or injury, and at times could have finished treatment, for example, on account of applying a mortar to a bit of hurt.

WHAT IS FIRST AIDS

First aid refers to the prompt care given to a person when harmed or sick until complete medical therapy is accessible. For minor circumstances, first aid care might be sufficient. First aid care ought to be gone on for significant issues until further developed care opens up.

The choice to act appropriately with first aid can mean the contrast between life and demise. Start by acquainting yourself with the harmed or sick person. Make sense that you are a first aid supplier and will help. The person should allow you to help them; don't contact them until they consent to be supported. Assuming that you experience a befuddled person or somebody who is harmed or sick, you can expect that they would believe you should help them. This is known as "suggested assent.

First aid is the first and prompt help given to any person experiencing a minor or significant sickness or injury, with care given to save a life, keep the condition from declining, or advance recuperation. It remembers starting mediation for an actual state preceding professional medical assistance being accessible, like performing cardiopulmonary revival (CPR) while hanging tight for an emergency vehicle and the total therapy of minor circumstances, for example, applying a mortar to a cut. First aid is by and large performed by somebody with basic medical training. Emotional wellbeing first aid expands the idea of first aid to cover psychological wellness. In contrast, mental first aid is utilized as early treatment for individuals in danger of treating PTSD. Struggle First Aid, zeroed in on safeguarding and recovering a singular's social or relationship prosperity, is being steered in Canada.

Numerous circumstances might require first aid, and numerous nations have regulation, guideline, or direction, which determines a base degree of first aid arrangement in specific conditions. This can incorporate explicit training or hardware to be accessible in the work environment (like a mechanized outer defibrillator), the collection of expert first aid cover at public social occasions, or compulsory first aid training inside schools. First aid, in any case, fundamentally requires no specific hardware or earlier information and can include the act of spontaneity with materials accessible at that point, frequently by undeveloped individuals.

IMPORTANCE OF FIRST AIDS

In the state, when somebody is wiped out or harmed, they frequently need assistance. First aid is the prompt medical consideration that can save a person's life, keep what is happening from deteriorating, or assist somebody with recuperating rapidly. Medical experts are completely prepared in first aid; however, different careers prescribe or expect representatives to know basic first aid. Instructors are genuine models. Whether it isn't needed for your work, realizing first aid can be very painful.

IT CAN SAVE A PERSON'S LIFE

First aid is significant because it can save somebody's life. There are numerous medical crises where there isn't a moment to spare. A wiped out or harmed person will most likely be unable to hold tight lengthy enough until experts show up, particularly on the off chance that it's challenging for personnel to contact them. If somebody there knows first aid, they can save the person's life by giving support like CPR.

IT EASES TORMENT

Most medical crises include torment. Indeed, even non-perilous occasions can be damaging due to the aggravation they cause. Somebody who realizes first aid can give that prompt help with discomfort. That can incorporate giving the person torment medicine from a first aid unit, setting up a moment initiating cold pack, pouring virus water over a consume, etc. Somebody prepared in first aid will know the appropriate help with discomfort techniques for explicit circumstances.

IT CAN FORESTALL CONTAMINATION

When somebody is harmed, how they treat that injury can improve or diminish the probability of contamination. Without legitimate training, compounding the situation is simple. For instance, many individuals believe it's OK to utilize hydrogen peroxide to disinfect a cut. This solid compound causes harm to the cells attempting to mend the injury. With the proper training and supplies (clean wraps, clean water, cleanser, oil jam, and so forth), you can advance mending and avoid contamination.

YOU CAN ALL THE MORE LIKELY CONVEY TO EXPERTS WHAT OCCURRED

If you know first aid and a person experiences a crisis, you can remain with them and assist immediately. When the experts show up, you are also better prepared to make sense of what occurred. The person experiencing the crisis may not be in that frame of mind to convey, yet you can give fundamental data about what prompted the situation and what it resembled. This correspondence assists the experts in pursuing the ideal choices for their patients.

IT MAKES WORKING ENVIRONMENTS MORE SECURE

The more individuals who know first aid in the working environment, the more secure it is. Medical crises can occur whenever, and if by some stroke of good luck one person knows first aid, what happens on the off chance that they're the ones experiencing the crisis? Multiple work environments likewise work with the general population, so realizing first aid assists a business with guarding their clients. You can alter your first aid training in light of the crises probably going to occur. For instance, if you work in a café, somebody could consume themselves, cut themselves, or stifle. Assuming you work outside in development, drying out and heatstroke are more probable, particularly in warm environments.

WHY BASIC FIRST AID KNOWLEDGE IS ESSENTIAL

There are various motivations behind why individuals don't take First Aid training programs;

They are excessively occupied

They feel that they, as of now, have sufficient information, or

They imagine that mishaps happen to others, not to them or their companions, family, and partners.

Ask any person who has taken a first aid training program on the off chance that it was worth the effort, and their response will be "Yes!" Having some basic first aid information is fundamental, and the following are five justifications for why.

IT ACCOMPLISHES MORE THAN ASSISTS WITH SAVING LIVES.

The realities affirm that having emergency treatment preparation, beyond question, makes a difference save lives. That is not all, however; giving suitable first aid promptly can assist with decreasing a person's recuperation time and affect the patient having a brief or long-term handicap. You'll figure out how to resist the urge to panic in crisis circumstances, and you'll learn short abbreviations to assist you with reviewing the means you need to take. First aid training will make you confident and agreeable and, along these lines, more powerful and in control when you should be.

IT EMPOWERS YOU TO INCREASE PATIENT SOLACE.

Not all mishaps, wounds, or sicknesses require an excursion to the emergency clinic; however, it doesn't mean they don't cause agony and experience the patient. A youngster crying due to a swollen elbow or with a fever is in torment and is languishing. By knowing the proper behavior - even by simply utilizing straightforward strategies, for example, applying an ice pack accurately or using suitable wrapping, you'll assist with easing their inconvenience. You'll likewise offer close-to-home help by keeping quiet and gathered, which will cause them to have a solid sense of reassurance and lessen their nervousness levels.

IT GIVES YOU INSTRUMENTS TO KEEP WHAT IS GOING ON FROM BECOMING MORE REGRETTABLE.

In specific circumstances, if a patient doesn't get primary first aid care quickly, their case will break down - frequently quickly. By having the option to give primary consideration, you can settle a patient until crisis clinical benefits show up. You'll figure out how to involve basic family things as devices on the off chance that a first aid kit isn't accessible, implying that you'll have the option to adapt to numerous circumstances.

You'll likewise be prepared on how to gather data and information about what occurred and the patients' condition. This data will be given to the crisis administrations, which saves them time - you will be an essential connection in the endurance chain.

IT MAKES THE CERTAINTY TO MIND.

Having basic first aid information implies that you'll be sure about your abilities and capacities corresponding to first aid organization. Taking first aid preparation assists you with considering yourself and how you and others respond in specific circumstances. This understanding will support your trust in a broad scope of non-clinical everyday events.

IT SUPPORTS SOLID AND SAFE LIVING.

Quite possibly, the earliest thing you will master during your first aid preparation is that you should care for yourself and guarantee your well-being as really important. It's not being egotistical, and it's being helpful. Protecting yourself implies you are in a situation to help other people instead of requiring help yourself. Likewise, you will find out about the significance of solid living and how the way of life propensities and decisions can increment or decline your dangers of creating issues like coronary illness. This information makes you more mindful of your wellbeing and cautious of potential risks presented by your environmental elements.

WHAT IS A FIRST AID KIT

A first aid kit is a crate, sack, or pack that holds supplies used to treat minor injuries, including cuts, scratches, consumption, injuries, and injuries. More intricate first aid kits can likewise incorporate endurance supplies, life-saving crisis supplies, or accommodation things like bug sting wipes or cold and influenza medications.

People who need to plan for health-related crises or, on the other hand, if they have a physical issue, will need to have the fitting first aid supplies prepared to utilize. This book provides you with a thought of the kinds of injuries to plan for and a rundown of the supplies used for every wound. There is a stockpile list of basic first aid kits that can be utilized for the injuries depicted. Whenever the situation allows, look for clinical consideration for any genuine injuries.

No one can tell when you could have to give basic first aid. Consider putting away a very much-supplied first aid kit in your home and vehicle to plan for the erratic. It's likewise brilliant to have a first aid kit accessible at work.

You can purchase preassembled first aid kits from many first aid associations, drug stores, or open-air diversion stores. On the other hand, you can make your first aid kit utilizing items bought from a drug store.

A standard first aid kit ought to include:

- glue wraps of arranged sizes
- roller swathes of arranged sizes
- spongy pack dressings
- sterile bandage cushions
- glue material tape
- three-sided wraps
- sterile wipes
- headache medicine
- acetaminophen or ibuprofen
- anti-infection salve
- hydrocortisone cream

- calamine salve
- nitrile or vinyl gloves
- self-locking pins
- scissors
- tweezers
- thermometer
- breathing boundary
- moment cold pack
- cover
- first aid manual

It's likewise savvy to incorporate a rundown of your medical care suppliers, crisis contact numbers, and recommended drugs in your first aid kits.

SOME INJURIES AND WHAT FIRST AID SUPPLIES TO USE

TRAUMA INJURIES

Horrible injury is a term that refers to actual injuries of unexpected beginning which require prompt clinical consideration. The affront might cause absolute shock called "shock injury" and may need quick revival and mediations to save life and appendage. Horrible injuries result from a wide assortment of obtuse, entering, and consuming components. They incorporate engine vehicle impacts, sports injuries, falls, catastrophic events, and many other actual injuries that can happen at home, in the city, or while at work and require prompt attention.

MINOR INJURIES

Minor injury implies an injury or other explicit harm to the body. For example, however not restricted to scraped spots, splinters, chomps that don't break the skin, and injuries.

Models:

Cuts and Scratches

Minor Consumes

Minor Eye Disturbances -

Hyper-extends and Strains

Eye injuries

Healthy skin Related Injuries

These are injuries that go through the skin to the fat tissue—brought about by a sharp item. Scratches, scraped spots, blemishes, and floor consumption. These are surface injuries that don't go through the skin.

Run-of-the-mill skin-related sicknesses incorporate burns from the sun, poison ivy, hives brought about by hypersensitive responses and bug stings. A large portion of these is effectively treated by utilizing over-the-counter salves. Consume gel is helpful for minor sun-related burns, while poison ivy can be treated with unique cured washed and creams. Bug nibbles usually are innocuous and can be treated with bug wipes or an allergy med like Benadryl. A specialist ought to see genuine responses that confine breathing or include enlarging.

HERE ARE WHAT FIRST AID "MUST-KNOWS" THAT YOU CAN USE TO TREAT A BROAD ARRAY OF INJURIES:

1. Remember the "Three P's."

2. Check the scene for risk before you assist.

3. To treat cuts and scratches, apply delicate strain, sanitizer, and gauzes.

4. Treating Sprains

5. To treat heat weariness, utilize cool liquids, excellent fabrics, and shade.

6. To treat hypothermia

7. Treating Burns

8. Allergic Reactions

Regardless, these basic first aid methodology can go quite far in aiding somebody who's injured, and you should simply involve a couple of materials in your endurance kit and perfectly apply them.

1. THE "THREE P'S."

The "Three P's" are the essential objectives of first aid. They are:

• Preserve life

• Prevent another injury

• Prepare for recuperation

These objectives could appear to be excessively straightforward. However, they're basic deliberately. When somebody is injured, it's all-too-simple to overreact and forget how you need to give help. The Three P's help you to remember the very basics:

• Give your best to save the individual's life.

• Give your very best to hold them back from supporting further injuries.

• Give your best to assist them with mending.

2. CHECK THE SCENE FOR RISK BEFORE YOU ASSIST.

Before assisting an injured individual, you should look at the scene for risk. You would instead not get yourself injured, as well. This is undoubtedly not fearful insurance. The truth is this: on the off chance that you get hurt, you will not have the option to help another injured person.

For instance, there may be a horrible storm outside, and you spot somebody outside who's injured and can't come to protect. Before you go running out to help them, search for risks. Are solid breezes heaving garbage? Are there any trees or designs that look like they're going to fall? Are there brought down electrical cables? Is there floodwater?

Whenever you've surveyed these risks, you can better plan how to reach and protect the injured individual.

3. TO TREAT CUTS AND SCRATCHES, APPLY DELICATE STRAIN, SANITIZER, AND GAUZES.

Blood is an indispensable part of our bodies. At a point when somebody is dying, you need to forestall however much blood from leaving their body as could be expected. Attempt and track down a perfect material or swathe. Then, at that point:

• Apply delicate tension for 20 to 30 minutes.

• Clean the injury by delicately running over it. Try not to utilize a cleanser on a fresh injury.

• Apply anti-toxin to the injury, similar to Neosporin.

• Cover the injury with a wrap.

The body is typically extremely fast at fixing up little cuts and scratches. In any case, further injuries might require clinical consideration. With profound injuries:

• Apply pressure.

• Look for clinical consideration quickly.

4. TREATING SPRAINS

Sprains are usually an unalarming injury, and more often than not, they'll recuperate all alone. In case there are steps you can take to facilitate the enlarging. Expanding is brought about by the bloodstream to a harmed region. You can decrease enlarging by applying ice. Ice limits the veins, which reduces the bloodstream.

• Keep the harmed appendage raised.

• Apply ice to the harmed region. Try not to apply ice straightforwardly to the skin. Enclose it with a material or put ice in a plastic pack.

• Keep the harmed region packed. Put it in support or firmly wrap it. Try not to wrap it so close that it'll remove a course.

• Ice for some time. Then pack. Rehash at intervals.

Ensure the harmed person tries not to put weight on the harmed appendage.

5. TO TREAT HEAT WEARINESS, UTILIZE COOL LIQUIDS, EXCELLENT FABRICS, AND SHADE.

Heat fatigue happens because of delayed openness to high temperatures, mainly when someone is doing challenging exercises or hasn't had sufficient water. Side effects of intensity fatigue include:

• Cool, clammy skin

• Weighty perspiring

• Tipsiness

• Powerless heartbeat

• Muscle cramps

• Queasiness

• Migraines

To treat somebody with heat fatigue:

• Get the person to a concealed region out of the sun.

• Assuming there are no concealed regions accessible, keep the person covered by any suitable materials that can obstruct daylight.

• Provide water for the person and keep them hydrated.

• Put a cool fabric on their time to bring down their internal heat level.

6. TREATING HYPOTHERMIA

Hypothermia is caused by delayed openness to cold temperatures. When your internal heat level dips under 95 degrees Fahrenheit, it starts to happen.

Side effects of hypothermia include:

• Shuddering

• Slurred discourse or murmuring

• Week beat

• Feeble coordination

• Disarray

• Red, cold skin

• Loss of awareness

To treat hypothermia:

• Be gentle with the distressed person. Try not to focus on their bodies and don't move their bodies excessively, jolting away; this could set off heart failure.

• Move the person out from the cold, and take off any wet apparel.

• Cover the person with covers and use heat packs. Try not to apply heat straightforwardly to the skin since this could cause significant skin harm.

• Give the person warm liquids.

Assuming you set the individual on the ground, know that the environment may likewise be a virus source. Put warm materials on the ground that the person will lay on.

7. TREATING BURNS

Before you apply treatment to burns, you need to identify the burn type and the seriousness of the burn. There are four sorts of burns:

• Severe singeing: Just the external layers of skin are burnt. The skin is red and enlarged and seems to be like a sunburn.

• Severe singeing: A portion of the inward layer of skin is burnt. Search for rankling skin and expanding. This is typically an exceptionally excruciating kind of burn.

• Severe singeing: the inward layer of skin is all burnt. The injury has a whitish or darkened variety. Some severe roasting is so profound that there is no agony because the sensitive spots are obliterated.

• Severe singeing: A burn that has entered all tissues up to the ligaments and bones.

Furthermore, there are two sorts of burn severities: a minor burn and a significant burn.

• Minor burn: severe singeing and gentle severe singeing.

• Significant burn: Moderate severe singeing to severely charred areas.

Minor burns don't generally require comprehensive treatment, yet you could:

• Run cool water over the burdened region (stay away from frigid or freezing water).

• Break no rankles.

• Apply lotion over the area, similar to aloe vera.

• Keep the burned person out of daylight.

151

Significant burns are intense wounds that need clinical support. To help somebody who has experienced a considerable burn:

• Try not to apply ointments.

• Cover twisted with free materials to prevent contaminants from tainting it.

8. ALLERGIC REACTIONS

Allergic reactions happen when your body is overly sensitive to an unknown substance. Honey bee stings, specific food sources, or medication ingredients can cause allergic reactions. Hypersensitivity is a dangerous allergic reaction brought about by those mentioned allergens.

The ideal way to treat an allergic reaction is to utilize an EpiPen. EpiPen, or "epinephrine autoinjector," is a little ergonomic needle used to infuse epinephrine (adrenaline) into somebody experiencing an allergic reaction enormously. Epinephrine normally represses the impacts of the allergic reaction.

If somebody is experiencing an allergic reaction:

• Keep the person quiet. Inquire as to whether they utilize an EpiPen and have one with them.

• Have the person lie on their back. Keep their feet raised 12 inches.

• Ensure the person's clothing is free, so they're ready to relax.

• Try not to give them food, drink, or medication.

• If fitting, figure out how to infuse an EpiPen in somebody reacting.

• Stand by 5-15 minutes in the wake of utilizing an EpiPen. If the allergic reaction isn't curbed, a subsequent portion might be required.

It's essential to shield yourself from contagious diseases and perils while giving first aid. To assist with safeguarding yourself:

• Continuously check for dangers that could seriously jeopardize your wellbeing before moving toward a debilitated or harmed person.

• Keep away from direct contact with blood, upchuck, and other natural liquids.

• Wear defensive equipment, for example, nitrile or vinyl gloves while treating somebody with a severe injury or a breathing obstruction while performing salvage relaxing.

• Clean up with cleanser and water following giving first aid care.

Generally speaking, total first aid can prevent what is going on from deteriorating. On account of a health-related crisis, first aid could try and save the day-to-day existence. If somebody has a genuine physical issue or sickness, they ought to get follow-up care from a clinical expert.

WHY SHOULD YOU KEEP FIRST AIDS AT HOME WHEN DOCTORS ARE NOT AVAILABLE?

Accidents and wounds can happen anyplace - at home, while driving or while taking part in games. They are not wanted, yet they do occur. Thus, it is essential to be ready for such health-related crises.

Keeping a first-aid kit at home can assist you with answering really to normal wounds and crises.

HERE IS THE ADVANTAGE OF HAVING A FIRST-AID KIT AT YOUR HOME

1. TREAT WOUNDS RAPIDLY:

First-aid kits assist you with taking care of the health-related crises as fast as could be expected. A postponement of simply a solitary moment can cause hostile harm in an emergency. These kits offer essential and instant consideration for normal clinical wounds like wounds, burns, cuts, etc.

2. PICKERING WELLBEING CAN FABRICATE KITS CUSTOM FOR YOUR HOME:

Pickering Wellbeing first-aid kits are adjustable. Assuming you work in a specific specialty, we can construct a first-aid kit that contains appropriate crisis equipment. We give first-aid kits to a comprehensive exhibit of organizations and experts in the clinical business, police force, and numerous organizations throughout the Lower Central area.

4. LESS HAZARD OF DIFFICULTY:

An exceptional first-aid kit, generally speaking, can prevent further confusion with the injury or ailment. Keeping clinical equipment helpful can be savvy since it's doubtful an injury treated quickly with a first-aid kit will require complex attention later on.

5. VERY MINIMIZED BUNDLE:

First-aid kits contain every one of the essential clinical contents in an exceptionally conservative bundle. You can genuinely take a first-aid kit with you, whether you're voyaging or living/working in a bit of space. There's no reason not to keep one close!

6. KEEP ANTIBIOTICS INSIDE ARMS REACH:

In case of a cut, it's essential to involve antibiotics as quickly as time permits to prevent disease. Pickering Security First-Aid Kits contain fundamental antibiotic ointments to be utilized in crises.

7. STOP BLOOD MISFORTUNE RIGHT AWAY:

Now and then, wounds are muddled. Applying dressing and gauze quickly will stop the blood misfortune. It's challenging to stop blood misfortune efficiently without legitimate clinical items nearby, and delayed blood misfortune can be hazardous.

BOOK 9: INTRODUCTION TO SURVIVAL

It is trying to adapt to outrageous conditions. It isn't only survival in extreme earthbound conditions yet instead the need for execution in daily existence, occupation, and sports. Both survival and performance require adapting to explicit natural stressors by versatile organic cycles of different sorts: variation, acclimatization, acclimation, and adjustment. Variation addresses a developmental process because of regular determination over age, which brings about the outflow of specific qualities that advance capacities (hereditary transformation). It also happens throughout an organic entity's life length, where specific organ capacities are required (phenotypic adaptation). Acclimatization is started by openness to outrageous indigenous habitats of beforehand not-uncovered people. It happens progressively inside the space of days to weeks, now and again even months, empowering execution support. Rather than acclimatization, acclimation includes versatile cycles prompted by openings to living rooms, where explicit kinds of outrageous circumstances are mimicked to accomplish acclimatization for later openness to usually happening absurd natural surroundings. At long last, adjustment characterizes the most common way of decreasing physiological and mental pressure reactions upon rehashed upgrades, i.e., further developed resistance. Changes incorporate physiological, morphological, and social responses, of which in the accompanying, a few short models will be given.

NECESSITIES FOR SURVIVAL

What necessities are fundamental for survival? Asylum, intensity, and dress will probably be among the central 10. And keeping in mind that these are advantageous and will make what is happening more agreeable, these are not fundamental. There are just four things a body needs to get by water, food, oxygen, and a working nervous system by the day's end.

1. WATER

Water is something beyond a refreshment. Pretty much every system in the body is reliant upon water in some shape or structure. The human body is roughly 60% water. Water controls body temperature and assists the liver and kidneys with flushing out poisons. Water greases up joints and saturates the eyes, nose, and mouth. Indeed, even oxygen and supplements are conveyed to cells by water. Without water, the body can't work. Individuals lose water by breathing, sweating, and, surprisingly, going to the restroom. To keep a healthy body, individuals need to recharge water levels and keep drinking water over the day. Direct water utilization is ideal. Refreshments, electrolyte beverages, and natural products, for example, watermelon, can assist with topping off the body's water supply. The standard suggestion is that ladies drink at least 11.5 cups of water daily and men 15.5 cups.

2. FOOD

Food gives fundamental supplements to the body. These supplements are utilized for energy, cell development, and fix. Food keeps the safe system cheerful, and, subsequently, terrible eating routines frequently lead to various medical conditions. Food can be separated into four fundamental gatherings: fats, carbs, protein, and nutrients. Fats give energy and assist with engrossing nutrients. Fats have some control over cholesterol levels and are fundamental for development and improvement. Sugars are switched over entirely to fuel. Fiber is a kind of carb that aids processing, directs glucose levels, and holds hunger levels under wraps. Protein assists the body with fixing harmed organs, tissues, and bones. Protein is tracked down in each cell in the human body. And keeping in mind that the body can deliver 12, there are as yet eight that should be eaten through food. Nutrients assume a part in each physical process. The human body needs 13 kinds of nutrients to work appropriately.

3. OXYGEN

Oxygen is breath. Life is beyond the realm of possibilities of all the other things saved without oxygen. Oxygen is breathed into the lungs and afterward scattered through the body by red platelets. Oxygen gives energy to cells by consuming the sugar and unsaturated fats that are consumed. The very red platelets that help oxygen through the body additionally do carbon dioxide of the body. Breathing out additionally eliminates carbon dioxide from the body.

4. THE NERVOUS SYSTEM

The nervous system is the body's war room. The nervous system gathers information, processes the data, and answers as needs be. The system controls development by communicating nerve driving forces between the cerebrum and the remainder of the body. The messages travel through neurons, neural connections, and synapses. These messages advise the heart to thump, lungs to inhale, and appendages to move. The nervous system even suggests to the cerebrum how to think. The nervous system has two sections: the focal and fringe. The jumpy focal system is comprised of the cerebrum and spinal rope. The fringe nervous system makes up the remainder of the body.

IMPORTANT TO STAY HEALTHY

Staying healthy has never been so exceptionally significant as the need to wait healthy can decidedly influence basically all aspects of our lives. Staying fit should be possible in various ways, including eating lean and healthy meats alongside many leafy foods.

Investing a little energy every day in practicing can help us become healthy and avoid the cutting-edge scourge of stoutness.

1. HELPS YOU LIVE LONGER

This is one of the clearest benefits of carrying on with a healthy lifestyle and is one of the essential reasons by far most hope to practice and eat a healthy eating regimen. Not set in stone to capitalize on their body as far as life span, there is an entire host of proof that connections stay healthy with longer life. One review ventured to such an extreme as to gauge the relationship between savoring liquor balance instead of smoking, practicing consistently, and eating a healthy eating regimen can stretch out your life by as long as 14 years.

2. FEEL BETTER ABOUT YOURSELF

One of the fundamental justifications for why staying healthy can help your life as you become older. One of the essential benefits is that continuing with a healthy lifestyle can cause you to feel more sure than in recent memory. Practicing can deliver chemicals to your cerebrum that upgrade your state of mind and give you a feeling of joy.

3. CONTROL YOUR PRESSURE

The cutting-edge world we live in is upsetting, with the capacity to turn off from work is a huge issue. One of the issues confronting us is how to deal with pressure with work out. The people who carry on with a healthy lifestyle have been demonstrated in clinical examinations to have lower levels of anxiety and tension.

4. KEEP AWAY FROM ADDICTIONS

Come, what sort of fixation you are impacted by a healthy lifestyle loaded up with exercise can restrict your longing for the drug. Whether your bad habit of decision is food, medications, or liquor, you will view it as a sprinter's high comparably habit-forming.

5. SAFEGUARD YOUR SIGHT

This may not be a significant part of carrying on with a healthy lifestyle. However, a healthy and legitimate eating regimen can safeguard your visual perception. Best vision as we age can be acquired with regular cardiovascular activity.

6. INCREMENT YOUR RICHNESS

If you are searching for a prolific future with bunches of kids, the exercise center is the spot to go. Studies by Harvard College scientists showed a higher sperm level among guys who practiced routinely.

7. THINK ABOUT YOUR CONFIDENCE

When you work out routinely, you will, as a rule, find you look and feel improved, prompting an ascent in your certainty. Higher Confidence can produce a seriously fulfilling life.

HOW TO STAY WARM, SAFE, AND HEALTHY WHEN IT GETS COLD

As we change from a delightful pre-winter climate into winter and the Christmas season, preventive wellbeing measures are a higher priority than at any other time.

1. RECEIVE AN IMMUNIZATION SHOT

With regards to seasonal influenza, anticipation is critical. Ensuring your family gets seasonal influenza immunization consistently is one of the main things you can do before joining the groups for Christmas shopping, gatherings, marches, and school plays.

2. TWEAK YOUR EATING ROUTINE

Eat for warmth, and eat for insusceptibility. Adding extra healthy fats, for example, olive oil, coconut oil, and nut and seed margarine, to your simple dinner plan can assist with stirring up your metabolic flames, which helps heal the body, as indicated by Columbia Wellbeing.

Continue to eat your healthy plate of mixed greens at lunch when your body is hottest, yet make the night dinner something warm to assist with keeping your body warm as the night progresses. Add warming flavors like cumin and paprika. Ginger is perfect for warming, and it supports the secure and stomach-related systems. Get imaginative with occasional mitigating and cancer prevention agent-rich food sources. Beets, pumpkins, winter squash, and yams help your security system and assist with safeguarding you from infections. Fill your sluggish cooker with feeding earthy colored rice, root vegetables, beans, and vegetables that can be frozen in little servings and immediately warmed for a warming bite.

A hot breakfast worked around moved oats, millet, and other entire grains gives quick warmth and copious complex sugars to fuel the body for the afternoon. Grains are plentiful in B nutrients and magnesium, which assist the thyroid and adrenal organs with directing body temperature during the freezing climate. Sprinkle cinnamon, nutmeg, or allspice on the cereal to help digestion and produce heat.

3. REMAIN HYDRATED

Keeping a decent food and water balance assists you with enduring the virus better. Drinking purified water helps your stomach-related framework, alleviates occasional stoppage, and keeps your skin hydrated when the dampness drops.

Even though you'd believe that a glass of red wine or spiked eggnog could warm you up quickly, liquor diminishes your center temperature. Research shows "liquor turns around certain reflexes that control internal heat level, particularly the body's capacity to shudder." It can likewise make you sweat, even in cool temperatures, which can additionally bring down your body's center temperature, seriously endangering you to hypothermia.

4. GET AN INCREDIBLE CONTINUE ON

Indeed, moderate activity is perfect for your general wellbeing. Yet, a review from the London School of Cleanliness and Tropical Medication found that people who practiced vivaciously for no less than over two hours per week "were around 10% less inclined to catch the influenza-like disease . . . moderate activity didn't appear to significantly affect seasonal influenza."

When winter shows up, attempt to get more cardio than expected with your family specialist's endorsement. Getting your heart to siphon quicker fortifies your heart and your resistant framework.

5. WATCH FOR HYPOTHERMIA

Assuming that you will do cardio outside in low temperatures, be ready for indications of hypothermia — strangely low internal heat level. Albeit the condition is probably at freezing temperatures, hypothermia can happen in modestly cool temperatures (above 40°F) if you become chilled from a spat the downpour or extreme perspiring.

In some cases, people with hypothermia don't understand they are experiencing the condition. A too-low internal heat level can influence the mind, leaving the individual with muddled thinking. Indications of hypothermia in grown-ups incorporate shuddering, disarray, slurred discourse, cognitive decline, and sluggishness.

6. DRESS PROTECTIVELY

Remain warm outside by dressing in layers, particularly when temperatures plunge beneath freezing. Protect yourself, and keep your center warm with an additional shirt or two under your breeze and a waterproof coat. Wear long clothing underneath your jeans.

Hypothermia frequently starts in the hands and feet, so keep your toes warm with thick fleece socks that offer general heat maintenance. Pick durable, protected shoes or boots to keep your feet dry and assist you with staying away from slips on smooth surfaces. Cover your head with a cap to forestall heat misfortune, and remember your hand-warming gloves or gloves.

WHAT IS ELECTRICITY?

Electricity is the progression of electrical power or charge. Electricity is both a fundamental piece of nature and one of the most generally utilized types of energy.

The electricity that we use is an optional energy source. It is delivered by changing over essential wellsprings of energy like coal, flammable gas, thermal power, solar system, and wind energy into electrical power. Electricity is likewise referred to as an energy transporter, which implies it may be switched over entirely to different types of energy like mechanical energy or heat.

SIGNIFICANT OF ELECTRICITY TO HUMANKIND

1 ELECTRICITY KEEPS PEOPLE WARM DURING WINTER

Before electricity, people required alternate ways of remaining warm throughout the colder time of year. In specific spots where the temperature decreased, it involved life and passing. People depended on chimneys, wood-consuming ovens, layers of attire, and the body heat of their friends and family. Remaining warm was regular work. With electricity, people can heat their homes with the turn of a dial.

2 ELECTRICITY HELPS PEOPLE COOK AND STORE FOOD

Electricity powers a broad scope of gadgets utilized for food prep and capacity. Before, people would cook over-consuming wood or coal, which required observing a ton. Present-day electric devices like broilers and microwaves are more advantageous and predictable. Saddling electricity additionally made ready for the development of coolers and coolers, which changed how people store food.

3 ELECTRICITY HEATS WATER

Contingent upon where you reside, your water heater is undoubtedly filled by electricity. Electric water heaters work by acquiring cold water through one cylinder, heating it with an electric heating component, and moving the water through your home with another line. If you have this kind of heater, and the power goes out, the water remains warm for a short period in light of the protected tank. Without a consistent electricity stock, you'll be washing up until the power returns on.

4 ELECTRICITY IS FUNDAMENTAL FOR CLINICAL CONSIDERATION

Medical care offices like emergency clinics rely upon reliable electricity. Lighting, security frameworks, cooling, electronic wellbeing records, and clinical gear need energy. Power blackouts are very difficult for medical services offices since they can't suspend their tasks; they can prompt the passing of patients. When blackouts happen, medical clinics and nursing homes frequently need to empty, which accompanies its dangers.

5 ELECTRICITY POWERS THE GADGETS WE UTILIZE EVERY DAY

A large portion of us use devices like PDAs and PCs consistently. They're required for keeping in contact with people, working, route, and diversion. There's a security factor, as well. If you don't have a PDA, it is a lot harder to find support in a crisis. Without electricity, you wouldn't have the option to charge these gadgets.

LIVE WITHOUT ELECTRICITY AND HOW TO MAKE YOUR ELECTRICITY

An existence without electricity in the advanced period can be a change. Even though it probably won't appear, there is still such a lot you can achieve without it and numerous elective energy sources to browse and introduce in your home.

ALTERNATIVE ENERGY

Concerning energy options, the main one that strikes a chord is solar power. Nonetheless, most solar boards won't work without electricity as they initially should take care of the power created back to the grid before driving your home can be utilized.

So if a power cut happens, solar-powered frameworks are futile without a completely working power grid. You can pick solar power frameworks that work off-grid and utilize giant battery banks to store the excess energy created. This can end up being exorbitant. However, if you have the spending plan and need to contribute, off-grid solar-powered frameworks are the least demanding and most solid course.

BATTERY CAPACITY

Batteries are at the core of any off-grid renewable energy source. Without storms putting away the energy created by renewable sources, your home would have the option to run on the power it gets at that time. The people who pick an off-the-grid way of life and create their renewable energy will ordinarily introduce battery power banks to store the excess energy delivered.

ALTERNATIVE HEATING

For those generally residing off the grid, they depend vigorously on wood-consuming ovens and chimneys for warmth as well as cooking. They are an incredible wellspring of heat for your home, and sharing the heat around rooms is simple. Nonetheless, it's memorable's critical to reserve dry wood for colder months.

Other elective heating strategies incorporate solar warmth and biomass, which are equipped to provide sufficient heat for a home.

HOW TO START A FIRE AND STAY WARM ALL THE TIME, EVEN IN FREEZING TEMPERATURES

I. START A FIRE

With winter weather at long last here in the country, it's wise to keep yourself prepared to light a fire. We aren't typically cautioned about forthcoming endurance circumstances, so it's essential to convey an EDC sack or endurance unit with us consistently.

On the off chance that there's consistently when it is essential, lighting a fire is in cold weather. The greatest endurance peril we face in the wintertime is hypothermia. Cold weather is terrible enough all alone, yet if you end up falling in a waterway or, in any case, getting wet, your possibilities of endurance drop from challenging to extremely very risky.

However, lighting a fire in cold weather isn't as simple as it is in warm weather. In addition to the fact that you are battling the troubles of weighty dress and your body being made firm from the cold, finding dry fuel and a decent spot for a fire are significantly more troublesome and neglected. Most fire-starters simply don't need to fill in as great when it's cold outside.

FINDING THE FIRE

Finding a decent area for your fire is significantly more basic in cold weather than at different times. Most importantly, the ground may not be dry. Things will be covered with snow, making it difficult to come by significant, clear areas. If they aren't covered with snow, you could find that everything you have is frozen ground. That won't function admirably, either, as the fire will liquefy the water in the environment, which will then, at that point, attempt to quench the fire.

DRY TINDER

The more pressing issue will be finding anything you can use as fuel. Tinder, by definition, is dry stuff. In any case, you won't find a lot of dry kinds of things around, except if you end up finding a neglected bird's home someplace.

Therefore our precursors conveyed a tinder box with them while voyaging. Instead of searching for fuel when it would be difficult to come by, they had the option to utilize the energy they were conveying with them. Then, at that point, when they found something that would function as fuel, they renewed their stock.

This is what you ought to do, also; convey your tinder with you. Whether as roast material or a business "fire-starter," having something that will promptly light with you guarantees your endurance. You could find all the other things you want in nature. However, if you can't find something to use as tinder, you will experience difficulty making a fire.

STARTING YOUR FIRE

This isn't the ideal opportunity for dazzling individuals with your capacity to light a fire by scouring two dry stays together. Nor is it an excellent opportunity to attempt to get two or three flashes from a Ferro Pole into some dry tinder. If you want an endurance fire in the winter, you can't bear to burn through any time. Disregard artfulness and go for the definite techniques for fire-beginning, matches, or a butane lighter.

II. STAY WARM

WEAR LAYERS

Wear a few layers of dress and strip them off on the off chance that you begin to get excessively hot. The intensity in the middle of between the layers keeps you decent and hot. I would suggest warm clothing as well. Of course, they're somewhat dorky; however, no one needs to see them, and they're shockingly hot despite their slim appearance. I credit this to one or the other, science or black magic.

SAFEGUARD YOUR CENTER

Keeping your center protected is the most brilliant thing to keep the remainder of your body warm during winter. The typical center temperature is 98.6 degrees Fahrenheit and hypothermia sets in when that temperature plunges under 95. There's a justification for why individuals right off the bat lose fingers, toes, and different furthest points to frostbite before whatever else. It's their body's usual type of self-protection. It quits sending blood out to these areas to safeguard crucial organs. So unusually, the best approach to keeping your fingers and toes warm, and joined to you, is by keeping your center hot.

Decent boots are essential to remain warm and prevent frostbite on the off chance that your shoes will be getting wet. The ideal choices are twofold boots, which contain a felt internal liner and a high-top external boot. They're warm and agreeable, yet entirely very costly. A less expensive choice might be a rugged mountaineering boot. It has comparable advantages to both fold boots, yet for a lower cost. Froth-protected rain boots will keep your feet warm yet make them sweat. This can be an issue, as we will find on our next trip.

STAY DRY

This may appear glaringly evident. However, the cold has a secretive approach to surprise you, especially on the off chance that you're presenting yourself to puddles, snow slush, or in any event, perspiring underneath the layers mentioned above. One method for keeping away from the last option is explicitly by putting resources into synthetic, wicker-based layers that pull the sweat right off your skin. If you get wet remotely, get inside and dry off as quickly as time permits.

HYDRATE

All carefully prepared mountain climbers witness how water is a fantastic method for holding body heat. The more you have in your framework, the simpler it is to keep warm. In light of this, ensure you stay hydrated in the winter and the mid-year, especially if you need to go out into the cold ordinary.

WHAT IS THE MATERIAL YOU NEED FOR SHELTERS?

While picking a spot to construct your shelter, attempt to remain close to a wellspring of water. If your situation is a crashed vehicle or a little plane, stay nearby the destruction as it is protected. If it's vigorously concealed from view, it remains nearby noticeable. Likewise, it would help if you avoided regular dangers like a dead braid that could fall, bluffs, and dry stream beds. Weighty downpours can transform a dry bed once more into a hurrying stream rapidly. Your shelter should be no greater than needed - - the bigger the shelter, the more challenging time you'll have held in the intensity.

If conceivable, don't rest straightforwardly on the ground. Heaping grass or pine needles can assist you in withholding body heat. Your shelter should be ventilated, particularly if you anticipate having a fire inside or close to the entrance. Utilize enormous shakes or tree limbs to obstruct the entryway. This prevents heat from getting out and creatures from getting in.

Simply recollect that in a crisis, your objective isn't solaced. It's to get past the night until you can evaluate what is happening and construct a legitimate shelter. It's additionally essential to be cautious while you're managing caves. Remain near the mouth, so you don't get lost, and be highly mindful of different animals looking for shelter nearby.

It's crucial in any endurance circumstance to utilize anything you find or, as of now, have with you. You can frequently find valuable materials abandoned by others. A touch of disposed grappling rope, some torn plastic sheeting, or even an old climbing boot can be of great use in the forest. You ought to continuously accumulate anything you have or find and keep it at your headquarters. Things like raincoats, nylon loungers, or parachutes can act as shelter materials.

If you have a raincoat or any sort of plastic sheeting, you can fabricate a few different kinds of shelters. What you need to do is imitate the state of a tent. For an essential shade shelter, everything you need to do is spread the material out to get under it. You can attach it between four trees to shape a covering if you have some rope. You can design a tent shelter by running string down the center of the rain guard between two trees, then, at that point, marking the sides into the ground with sharp sticks to make A-outline. One more basic shelter can be made by binds two inverse corners of the raincoat to trees. The opposite end slants askew to the ground and can be gotten with stick stakes or heavy rocks.

If you have no rope, construct a one-individual tent from tree limbs:

Take a forked tree appendage and wedge it about a foot down, with the "Y" facing up.

The ridgepole is the middle roof support and ought to be straight and strong. Run it starting from the earliest stage of the fork, resting in the "Y."

Make an "A" for the tent entryway by resting durable slanting branches inverse that meets at the fork. Use plant or dainty green branches to lash together each of the three to help focus. Make a ribbed casing with branches set corner to corner along the ridgepole, sufficiently wide, so you have space inside.

When you have your casing fabricated, wrap your cover over the top and stake it down with sharp sticks.

BOOK 10: 72-HOUR EMERGENCY KIT

PREPARE YOUR KIT THAT WILL ENABLE YOU TO SURVIVE AT LEAST FOR THE FIRST 72 HOURS WHEN THE DISASTER BEGINS

One of the principal disaster readiness steps is constructing a 72-hour emergency kit.

A 72-hour emergency kit contains all you need to endure the prompt eventual outcomes of a disaster.

Here we'll discuss why the 72-hour kit is so important, give you a plan, and a few choices for getting everything rolling.

If you are prepared to assume control over your wellbeing and survival, then, at that point, you should construct a 72-hour disaster readiness kit.

HERE ARE WHAT YOU WILL NEED:

WATER

It is one of the most fundamental components of life, and you can go three days without water before biting the dust.

Try not to count on your pipes to work after a significant disaster.

You should have something like 1 gallon of water for each individual each day stored. This is the base amount of water required for drinking, cooking, and essential cleanliness. If you have a group of four, you will require at least 12 gallons of water (3 gallons for every individual).

NOTE

Whether your pipes are working, it doesn't imply that it is protected to hydrate emerging from the tap!

The CDC cautions that water disinfection offices probably won't work when the power goes out. Avoid any risks and hydrate or clean your water. Additionally, focus on bubble alarms.

EMERGENCY TOILET

Many of us underestimate indoor pipes, so an emergency toilet isn't something that the vast majority contemplate until it is past the point of no return.

Salvage laborers during disasters recount accounts of entering homes where the toilet hasn't been flushed for quite a long time. You can envision what a clean (and foul) disaster can be!

Most toilets work on a gravity framework. Thus, regardless of whether you have running water, you can, in any case, flush the toilet by unloading a ton of water into the bowl (manual flush).

Therefore, you will need to have significantly more emergency water accumulated. It takes a gallon of water to flush the toilet physically. So you will need to store an additional 1-3 gallons of water for each individual each day.

It isn't generally smart to naturally flush your toilet during an emergency, especially when flooding or storms.

The ground can become immersed, which makes sewer frameworks flood. The CDC suggests restricting the amount of plumbing you use (washing garments, showering, flushing the toilet, etc.). If not, you could have a serious (and unhygienic) wastewater issue in your home through low-level channels!

Be ready by remembering an emergency toilet for your 72-hour disaster readiness kit.

SURVIVAL FOOD

You can go as long as 30 days without food; however, could you truly need to? If you have food to support yourself, you will endure the fallout of a significant disaster much better, both truly and mentally.

Canned foods are the clearest survival foods since they keep going for quite a while, are not difficult to store, and might endure flooding. In any case, remember that survival food ought likewise to be not difficult to plan.

I truly like freeze-dried food pockets since you simply have to add water and they are all set. Besides, freeze-dried food tastes significantly better compared to canned food.

Remember that there are different sorts of survival food (for example, survival foods for at home versus clearing). Find out about survival food here.

EMERGENCY WARMTH

How will you help warmth, assuming the lattice goes down around mid-? You would rather not be in a circumstance where you need to consume your furniture to remain warm.

Be ready by having an emergency radiator and fuel for it of some kind (truly, remember about the fuel!).

You will likewise need to have fleece covers in your home. Why fleece covers? Since they will, in any case, keep you warm in any event when they are wet. A wet cotton cover will simply make you colder.

FLASHLIGHTS AND EMERGENCY LIGHTING

It is great to have more than one sort of emergency lighting close by, like spotlights and candles. A few disasters (like EMP) could sear hardware like electric lamps.

Electric lamps can likewise break down when they get wet in flooding.

Remember about additional batteries for your spotlights! I, for one, really like to keep a battery-powered headlamp electric lamp in my 72-hour kit. Getting things done while wearing a headlamp than holding a spotlight in one hand is significantly more straightforward!

SANITATION AND HYGIENE ITEMS

Preparing isn't about food and water. You likewise need to ensure that you have sufficient toilet paper (which would give entirely different importance to SHTF!) and other essential cleanliness things. The fact that you ought to have amassed makes here some:

TOILET PAPER OR TOILET PAPER TABLETS

Child wipes (can be utilized to clean your body when you can't shower)

Anti-bacterial hand gel

Cleanser

Ladylike items (my better half purposes a feminine cup, so we don't need to store female items)

Diapers

Garbage sacks

EMERGENCY RADIO

A radio is significant for your 72-hour kit. By what other method would you say you should be aware if there are departure orders set up, whether all the more terrible weather conditions are coming, or other basic news?

An emergency radio should be waterproof and have a dependable power source. A hand-wrench radio is presumably an ideal choice. Numerous emergency radios have different highlights like inherent electric lamps as well.

BOARD-UP, CLEANUP, AND REPAIR SUPPLIES

Probably the most probable disasters incorporate quakes, twisters, and typhoons.

During these disasters, serious harm can happen to your home -for example, broken windows and rooftops being brushed off. Assuming you are caught in your home in the fallout of the disaster, how can you go to hold rain back from getting through the messed-up rooftop? How can you go to tidy up all that wrecked glass?

It is essential to keep some fundamental block, cleanup, and fix supplies in your 72-hour emergency kit.

EVACUATION KIT

At long last, remember to pack a cleaning kit that incorporates all of the essential stuff you will require on the off chance you need to escape your home.

Tragically, many individuals depend on living in fantasy land and try not to pack a departure kit (otherwise known as Bug Out Bag). Then, when compelled to escape, they need to run out within and won't sense anything except what last-minute things they can snatch.

IN YOUR EVACUATION KIT, YOU WILL NEED:

- Clearing documents
- Water + channel
- Survival food (Where to purchase modest MREs)

- Emergency cover
- Camping bed
- Change of garments
- Emergency treatment kit
- Prescriptions
- 72-Hour Emergency Kit Checklist
- Food and Water
- Durable food - See our manual for food protection
- 6 gallons of water for every individual (2 gallons each day) - See our manual for putting away water
- Can opener (non-electric) or study how to open a can without a can opener.
- Camp cooking oven and fuel
- Pots/skillet, utensils
- Emergency treatment, Hygiene, and Safety
- Emergency treatment kit
- Unscented bleach (around 5.25% chlorine for decontaminating water)
- Child wipes
- Hand sanitizer
- Substantial plastic packs
- Emergency toilet (two can framework suggested)
- Dispensable latex gloves
- Dust veil - (Guide to facemasks)
- Supply of physician-recommended meds - (Guide to fish antibiotics)
- Harm Mitigation
- Fire douser
- Window blockade (hammer, nails, wood boards)
- Wrench or pincers (for switching off utilities)
- Rock-solid gloves
- Bolt cutters
- Brush and dustpan
- Scoop
- For Sheltering in Place
- Six enormous canvases or plastic sheeting; 2ml least
- Channel tape
- 50 feet of nylon rope

- Spotlights or another off-lattice lighting (candles and open blazes ought not to be utilized after a quake because of the chance of gas spill!)
- Battery-controlled or hand wrench radio and an NOAA Weather Radio with tone alert
- Camping beds or fleece covers
- Change of garments and footwear for every individual
- Downpour coats or rain guards
- Additional batteries, ideally battery-powered with an off-lattice charging technique
- Sun-based power bank
- Survival lighter or fire starter
- Whistle or flagging strategy
- Emergency manuals (water sanitization, medical aid, shielding setup directions)

OTHER ITEMS

- Duplicates of essential documents put in a waterproof cover
- Solace things (games, books, toys for kids, etc.)
- Cash in little bills
- Pet supplies
- Additional keys for vehicle and house

WHY IS IT ESSENTIAL TO BE PREPARED FOR THE FIRST 72 HOURS?

Having 72 hours of provisions isn't sufficient to help you through a significant disaster. The most developed peppers have food supplies going 25+ years into what's to come. This isn't something that you develop for the time being.

To get to that level, you'll have a preparing spending plan, master numerous abilities, have a capacity and pivot framework, and realize things like how to store food appropriately.

Anyway

Having an adequate number of provisions for 72 hours will extraordinarily expand your possibilities of enduring an emergency.

Here are only a portion of the reasons a 72-hour kit is so important:

UTILITIES GO DOWN DURING DISASTERS:

You've presumably currently encountered this during storms. On the off chance that a little snowstorm or storm can take out the power for a long time, envision what will occur during a significant disaster! For instance, 8.1 million homes went without power after Hurricane Sandy, some of them for an entire month.

SUPPLIES RUN OUT:

Most individuals are ill-equipped, as is evident from those who race to the general store and equipment storm the day before a cyclone hits. On the off chance that the disaster takes out streets or traffic is confined, supply trucks will not have the option to restock supplies.

THE GOVERNMENT WON'T HELP:

We will not get into a political discussion about FEMA here, yet most Americans believe that the government will act as the hero after a disaster. They can be sure that it takes an average of 72 hours for state and central governments to answer. Their reaction is to aid the most pessimistic scenarios, similar to individuals caught under rubble, and circulate MREs to the majority pushing in line.

WOUNDS LEAD TO DEATH FOLLOWING 72 HOURS:

Wounds that appear minor can turn dangerous in no less than 72 hours if legitimate emergency treatment isn't regulated.

Void racks disaster readiness

Void store racks before Hurricane Sandy hit; Image credit: Wiki Commons

175

HOW WILL YOU ACCESS YOUR SUPPLIES IN CASE OF AN EMERGENCY?

Along these lines, you'll have the option to get to your 72-hour kit paying little heed to where you are when disaster strikes.

Ensure that the supplies are safeguarded against the elements - especially water.

I like to:

Put my center supplies in a fixed plastic sack, which I put inside a 5-gallon container.

You won't have the option to fit every one of your supplies in the container; however, ensure the ones helpless to water harm are secured.

Assuming that your supplies are spread by and large around the home (coats in the wardrobes, camping cots away, can opener in the kitchen), you will have the opportunity to assemble them all when disaster strikes.

You should keep all your crisis supplies in a single spot!

Where you keep your emergency kit will change contingent upon the sort of disaster you are preparing for. In a tropical storm region, you wouldn't want your disaster supplies in the basement (which will flood).

You don't want your disaster supplies with racking that could fall in that frame of mind in a seismic tremor zone.

Ideally, you keep your 72-hour kit in a similar spot where you will protect, for example, your basement, tornado cellar, or safe room.

Far and away superior, make more than one 72-hour kit and keep it in different areas. These are notwithstanding the emergency kits for your vehicle and work environment!

A 72-hour emergency kit is unquestionably the minimum that you ought to have. In a perfect world, each home will have supplies for 30 days and an objective to store a year of supplies.

If you are quite recently getting everything rolling with emergency readiness, fabricating a year of disaster supplies can be overpowering.

- Begin gradually
- Get the things in the 72-hour emergency kit agenda ASAP.
- Set a financial plan and use it every week to get a few additional supplies.
- Rather than throwing plastic jugs, clean them and fill them with water.
- Begin perusing guides on disaster readiness and endurance.
- Before long, you will be prepared for anything that disaster might strike!

HOW TO PREPARE FOR THE COMING ENVIRONMENTAL DISASTER, PREPARE YOUR SURVIVAL KIT (SUITCASES AND MEDICINE) WITH THE ESSENTIALS YOU NEED TO FACE THE EVENT

Disaster can strike whenever. Furthermore, since we can't decide when or where an emergency will occur, you and your family should be ready.

Your family genuinely should know how to answer what is going on, and an incredible device is a home emergency plan. A home emergency plan can keep your family individuals in total agreement, assist you with arriving at security, and limit frenzy and confusion.

Here are our top ways to make a home emergency plan to assist you with a beginning.

1. CONSIDER YOUR UNIQUE NEEDS.

Where you reside and the particular necessities of your family individuals are the central point to consider in your home emergency plan. Know what cataclysmic events could happen in your space and how best to plan for crises like tropical storms, serious flooding, volcanoes, or cyclones.

Furthermore, decide whether you need to make unique facilities for specific family individuals, like senior residents, family individuals with incapacities, infants, and small kids. Likewise, you ought to consider all individuals' clinical and dietary necessities from your family.

2. MAKE A DISASTER SUPPLIES KIT.

A disaster supplies kit is an extraordinary method for having all that you want in one spot so you can rapidly clear. Your kit should fit in a couple of simple to-convey packs and contain things to assist you with getting by all alone for no less than 72 hours.

At one time per year, audit what's in your emergency kit. Supplant lapsed things and update what you're bringing along as your family's requirements change.

3. KNOW WHERE TO GO.

Each emergency is different, so your place of refuge will fluctuate by circumstance. In the first place, find safe spots in your home for each circumstance where you would have to take cover, similar to a seismic tremor or twister. Second, find a gathering spot just external your home if there should be an occurrence of a fire or other emergency. Third, figure out where you c go if you are approached to empty or can't get back and plan the course you would take to arrive.

4. STAY CONNECTED.

Make a family correspondence plan. The plan ought to remember data for how you will get nearby emergency alarms (radio, TV, text, and so on) and data on the best way to stay in touch with one another.

Ensure all family individuals have emergency telephone numbers saved in their wireless and composed on a contact card. Incorporate numbers for every family part, the police headquarters, a close-by medical clinic, and an out-of-region emergency contact.

It might be more straightforward to contact somebody away, assuming an emergency influences your area, so it is shrewd to assign an out-of-region contact. Train all family individuals to stay in contact with this emergency contact to tell them that they are protected.

Likewise, assuming a disaster in your space, you can stamp yourself protected on Facebook or register on the American Red Cross Safe and Well site, so your friends and family realize that you're fine.

5. PROTECT YOUR PETS.

While planning for an emergency, remember about your pets! Make a rundown of pet-accommodating lodgings and creature covers along your departure course. Additionally, remember things for your pet for your disaster kit.

6. WRITE IT DOWN AND PRACTICE.

Ensure you write your emergency plan down with itemized guidelines for every circumstance. How you respond to a cyclone will differ from how you respond to a departure, so you should have a plan for everyone. Also, there are numerous web-based assets to assist you with documenting your plan, similar to this structure from the American Red Cross.

Practice your plans two times per year. You ought to try and snatch your emergency kit for departure drills and drive to your clearing course.

7. AUDIT YOUR PROTECTION.

Before a disaster strikes, it is savvy to survey your insurance contract with your agent to ensure you have the right inclusion for gambles in your space. For example, a standard home strategy normally does exclude securities like flood protection or tremor inclusion.

You likewise ought to ensure you know how to record a case, if important, whether through your transporter's misfortune revealing telephone line or site or through your agent.

While you may not know when a disaster will strike, you can breathe a sigh of relief with a home emergency plan and realize that your family is ready for whatever comes in your direction.

SAFETY STRATEGIES TO PROTECT YOUR FAMILY BY ANY MEANS NECESSARY

However, the greatest dangers to somewhere safe are exceptionally close and personal. As per the National Safety Council (NSC), engine vehicle accidents, falls, accidental harming, suffocating, and stifling are the main sources of unintentional demise in the United States. Try not to disregard the absolute least demanding ways of guarding your family. These ten hints can help.

1. LOCK-IN. In the event of a fender bender, this basic demonstration can mean the contrast between life and demise. As per the NSC, engine vehicle crashes are the main Source of death for individuals ages 1 to 33. In about 12 1/2 minutes, somebody in the United States is killed because of a car accident. Like clockwork, somebody experiences a crippling physical issue. Safety belts save the existence of thousands of individuals consistently.

2. USE YOUNGSTER SECURITY SEATS. Utilizing a youngster security seat can diminish the gamble for lethal injury by about 70 percent in kids under age 1. Ensure to introduce the seat appropriately — nearly 80 percent are not introduced accurately. The secondary lounge is the most secure spot for a kid's well-being seat. If a kid should ride in the front seat, the airbag should be switched off. For more data on the best way to introduce vehicle seats, visit the National Highway Traffic Safety Administration.

3. TRY NOT TO DRIVE UNDER THE INFLUENCE. Think about this: Approximately 40 percent of car accident deaths include drinking. More than 60 percent of the youngsters ride in alcoholic driver's vehicles in tanked driving deaths, including kids. The NSC says that about three in each 10 Americans will be associated with a liquor-related car crash eventually in their lives. If you will drink, assign a nondrinker to drive. On the other hand, flag down a taxi.

4. WEAR A HEAD PROTECTOR. Continuously utilize a head protector while trekking or playing sports, like football, hockey, or baseball. The NSC says around 800 bicyclists bite the dust every year in crashes, including engine vehicles. A head injury frequently brings about irreversible harm to the mind. Wearing a cap can cut the gamble for head injury by around 85%. Authorize severe principles with your children — no protective cap, no playing the game or trekking. Set a genuine model by wearing your head protector while trekking.

5. PREVENT FALLS. Over 50% of all falls happen in the home. The CDC reports that around 20,000 individuals aged 65 and more seasoned kick the bucket every extended time of falls.

Children are nearly as likely as seniors to be harmed in a fall, yet you can do whatever it takes to assist with keeping both more seasoned grown-ups and children securely upstanding. Keep your home clear of stumbling perils, like electrical strings, area rugs, and toys on the floor. Keep steps liberated from mess and put handrails on both sides, everything being equal. Introduce light switches at the top and lower part of the steps. Utilize nonslip mats in the bath and shower. Introduce snatch bars close to the restroom and in the tub or shower.

Never let a child be on a bed or changing table, and utilize the safety belts on high seats and carriages. Introduce doors to prevent admittance to flights of stairs and overhangs. What's more, make sure axles on flights of stairs are four inches separated or less to prevent a newborn child's head from falling through them.

6. WATCH THOSE WINDOWS. Screens are intended to store bugs out, not children. If you introduce monitors that hold children back from opening windows over a couple of inches, make sure that the guards can be delivered effectively in a fire. Intermittently look at your windows to ensure they're not painted, nailed, or enlarged shut.

7. PREVENT HARM. The NSC says that harm is a main source of death. Individuals at the most elevated risk for harm at home are 25 to 44. The principal substances that cause incidental demise are prescriptions, toxic houseplants, cleaning items, and pesticides. Keep your prescriptions locked away from curious youthful fingers and consistently fix kid-safe covers appropriately. Move your cleaning items to cupboards with wellbeing locks. Keep your nearby toxin control focus telephone number near the telephone.

8. BE VIGILANT WHEN CLOSE TO WATER. More than 3,000 individuals suffocate consistently, and children up to progress in years 4 are the most vulnerable. Never let your youngster be at a pool, ocean side, or bath. If you have a pool, close it in, introduce self-shutting entryways prompting it and put toys away from curious eyes when not being used. For added security, introduce a cover that prevents admittance to the water.

9. HOLD CHILDREN BACK FROM GAGGING. Suffocation is a main source of death in the home for children ages four and more youthful. Continuously put infants to bed on their backs on a solid sleeping pad, not on a delicate pad, cushion, or cover. Keep plays with long ropes and window-conceal pull lines from little children. Children under four can stifle on firm, round food sources. Like popcorn, nuts, grapes, and hard treats, present new food varieties cautiously. Likewise, keep little items that a youngster could swallow — like gems and tacks — securely unattainable.

10. BE READY FOR THE FIRE. Smoke alarms and fire quenchers can assist with preventing injury and passing if a fire breaks out in your home. Test smoke alarms month to month and change the batteries twice per year. Ensure everybody knows where to meet external the house and show children their last name, address, and how to call 911 in a crisis. To assist with preventing fires at home, make sure all electrical machines, electrical ropes, and outlets are looking great; keep children, pets, and ignitable materials from space warmers; assuming you smoke, don't smoke in that frame of mind on upholstered furniture.

SAFETY STRATEGIES TO PROTECT YOURSELF BY ANY MEANS NECESSARY

1. SECURE YOUR PREMISES. Personal well-being at home begins with getting your property and assets. The ideal way to make sure you and your family stay protected from dangers at home is to put resources into a checked home security framework. A security framework will give you 24/7access to who is entering (or attempting to enter) your home. To shield your possessions from excluded visitors, you should avoid giving out your home location, appropriately secure your home - entryways, windows, locks, and so on - and put resources into planned personal property inclusion.

2. STAY UNDER THE RADAR AT HOME AND ONLINE. Avoid any danger to your home or family by keeping a safe position.

At home: Steer clear of showing plain images at your home that could demonstrate a cop lives there. Avoid driving stamped vehicles home or leaving them in your carport, change into regular citizen garments when off the clock, and enroll reliable neighbors to watch out for dubious vehicles or walkers.

Online: Do not put your area of expertise name or identification number online. Be careful of posting any photographs of yourself in your uniform on any personal profiles, and never give out any personal information to anybody on the web.

3. SPEAK WITH YOUR LOVED ONES. However much you might attempt to protect your mate and children from dread and stress, it's vital to make and share a well-being plan with them. Plunk down together and examine what to do (or not do) if they feel hazardous or assume they experience a danger online.

Likewise, you can go to lengths to guarantee your family's well-being, similar to area following and telephone observing applications.

4. UTILIZE WEB-BASED ENTERTAINMENT ASTUTELY. The web has made it simple for unfriendly people to find personal information about cops and their families and interaction known as dozing. The information they uncover can be utilized to pester officials and their relatives online and face to face.

The most effective way to manage to doze is to be wise about what you share via web-based entertainment. Avoid posting in uniform, never share personal information, and advise your family to be careful about what they are sharing.

Should badgering happen through any web-based entertainment stage, make a quick move and report to these outlets regarding your commandants.

5. AVOID IDENTITY THEFT. Identity theft is an undeniable danger to American purchasers.

Identity theft happens when your recognizable personal information (PII) becomes compromised. Distinguish theft can happen to anybody at any stage in life and destroy your credit. ID theft tricks and fake joblessness guarantee tricks are rising during the pandemic. To avoid identity theft, this is what you can do:

Never share Social Security numbers, PINs, and other numeric information connected to your identity and logins.

Try not to place charge card numbers in messages.

Avoid opening messages you don't have the foggiest idea, and never click on connections or connections except if you should rest assured that they are authentic.

Utilize perplexing and extraordinary passwords for every one of your online records that blend letters, numbers, and typographic images in upper and lower case.

Try not to utilize birthday events, commemorations, or pet names.

Avoid online tests requesting realities about your life occasions and inclinations.

California Casualty offers all policyholders admittance to liberate ID theft goals administrations from CyberScout. On occasion, you or a relative has theirs recognized, taken, and utilized for deceitful exchanges. The help can assist with restricting harm, assembling proof against fraudsters, and reestablishing harmed credit.

6. SAFEGUARD YOUR FINANCES. While checking your credit for any progressions or indications of identity theft, you should watch out for each of your monetary records for dubious movement. You ought to look at balances on every one of your records as frequently as workable for any changes. Furthermore, on the off chance that your supplier offers dubious action alarms, join! However, know - some phone tricksters act like charge card organizations that will call you to attempt to get your record information. Never give anybody your personal information or Visa number via telephone, regardless of whether they guarantee they are with your supplier. Hang up and check for yourself.

7. PLAN FOR YOUR FUTURE. Having an insurance contract set up from a believed supplier can assist with moderating the staggering monetary difficulties families can look after a car collision, robbery, catastrophic event, or more. California Casualty has been safeguarding cops since 1969 and offers limited rates and selective advantages, including off-the-clock gun inclusion and the Fallen Hero benefit.

It is a lamentable reality that individuals committed to safeguarding society are confronting these dangers themselves; however, cops are no aliens to risk. As usual, remain safe and be ready.

BOOK 11: MENTAL HEALTH SURVIVAL GUIDE

HOW TO COPE WITH AND OVERCOME STRESS, ANXIETY, DEPRESSION, AND ALL THE NEGATIVE EMOTIONS THAT BOTHER YOU DURING DIFFICULT TIMES

Stress is the body's reaction to physical or close-to-home requests. Close-to-home stress can assume a part in causing depression or be a side effect of it. A stressful circumstance can set off sensations of depression, and these sentiments can make it harder to manage stress.

High-stress events, for example, losing employment or the conclusion of a drawn-out friendship, can prompt depression. Not every person who encounters these circumstances becomes discouraged. Organic variables might explain why one individual confronting a stressful situation encounters depression while someone else doesn't.

CAUSES OF STRESS

Losing a relative, separating, and moving are significant life changes that can cause stress. A few examinations Believed Source connect an overactive stress framework and elevated degrees of cortisol in the body to depression and other medical issue, including coronary illness. When the brain feels compromised, the body creates more stress chemicals — like cortisol — to help the body battle or take off from the danger. This functions admirably assuming that you're in genuine peril; however it doesn't necessarily, in every case, benefit you in your routine.

Different instances of events that can cause stress include: getting into a battle with your mate or critical other, losing your employment, significant catastrophic events, like tremors or twisters, that can harm your home or obliterate it, and out getting into a fender bender, which can cause physical, profound, and monetary stress being burglarized, robbed, or went after

A certain way of life decisions can likewise add to your stress levels. This is particularly evident assuming they influence your general well-being or, on the other hand, if you become reliant upon unfortunate survival strategies. Way of life decisions that can expand your stress include weighty or unnecessary utilization of liquor, not getting sufficient activity, smoking or utilizing unlawful medications working for significant periods without having some time off, or being an "obsessive worker" not eating an even eating regimen investing an excess of energy to sitting in front of the TV or playing computer games taking a gander at a cell phone in bed, which can hold you back from nodding off In some cases the consistent stresses of day to day existence trigger your survival reaction. This can prompt difficulties, including depression. In different cases, the advancement of depression is irrelevant to stress.

Depression can make encountering and adapt to events in your day-to-day existence seriously testing. Of all shapes and sizes, stresses happen; however, with depression, you may not feel as furnished to manage them. This can make the side effects of depression and the stress of specific circumstances surprisingly more terrible.

TYPES OF STRESS

Stress can be brought about by a solitary occasion or by impermanent circumstances. This is known as intense stress. Intense stress can be welcomed by events that stress you out, like stepping through a major exam or an intense injury, like a wrecked bone.

Stress can likewise keep going for quite a while, never feeling like it's backing off. On these occasions, events or ailments might cause persistent stress, or there might be no great explanation for your stress. This is known as chronic stress. Chronic stress is typically the aftereffect of an individual, way of life, or medical problems likewise chronic. Normal reasons for chronic stress include:

• Having monetary battles

• Working at a high-pressure work

• Having individual or relationship issues at home

• Not feeling like you have sufficient help from family or companions

EFFECTS OF STRESS ON DEPRESSION

While stress can, for the most part, adversely affect your physical and emotional well-being, it tends to be particularly unsafe assuming that you have depression.

Stress can cause you to feel less ready to keep up with good propensities or survival methods, which are vital to overseeing depression. It can cause the side effects of depression to feel more extreme. Intruding in a solid routine can bring about negative survival techniques, like drinking or pulling out of social connections. These activities can bring about additional stress, which can then aggravate depression.

Stress can likewise influence your mindset, as uneasiness and peevishness are normal reactions to stress. When a stressor makes you restless, the uneasiness might bring about additional negative sentiments or disappointment, regardless of whether the stressor is short-term.

TIPS ON MANAGING STRESS

Stress the executive's procedures help adapt to depression. Stress alleviation can likewise assist with keeping burdensome side effects from creating. Some accommodating stress the executive's strategies include:

• Getting sufficient rest

• Eating a solid eating regimen

• Getting customary activity

• Taking periodic get-aways or customary breaks from work

• Tracking down a loosening up side interest, like cultivating or carpentry

• Polishing off less caffeine or liquor

• Doing breathing activities to bring down your pulse

Assuming way of life decisions are causing you stress, you might consider impacting how you approach your own or proficient life. A few different ways you can assist with diminishing this sort of stress include:

• Putting yourself under less strain to perform at work or school, for example, by settling for the easiest option to a level you view as OK

• Not taking on as numerous obligations at work or exercises at home

• Sharing liabilities or assigning errands to others around you

• Encircling yourself with strong and positive loved ones

• Eliminating yourself from stressful conditions or circumstances

Exercises like yoga, contemplation, or going to strict administration can likewise assist you with managing stress. A blend of these procedures might demonstrate considerably more success. It's critical to find what works for you. Also, regardless of anything you pick, it's indispensable to have dear loved ones who will uphold you.

Conversing with an instructor, specialist, or other emotional wellness experts can likewise be a helpful method for managing stress and depression. Talk treatment alone or joined with mental, social treatment (CBT) or drug is a demonstrated answer for both depression and chronic stress. Prescriptions for depression include:

• Particular serotonin reuptake inhibitors (SSRIs, for example, citalopram (Celexa)

• Monoamine oxidase inhibitors (MAOIs), like isocarboxazid (Marplan)

WHAT THE EXPERT SAYS

"A discouraged individual is compromised in managing risky circumstances," says Stacey Stickley, an authorized proficient guide rehearsing in Ashburn, Virginia. "At the stage when an individual is managing depression, things might appear to be more negative than they truly are. Events that would have been accepted may appear more tricky or difficult to deal with. Making a move on things might require to a greater extent an individual's assets, assets that are as of now compromised because of the depression."

Converse with your primary care physician about pharmacological choices, or search for a guide about assessing and dealing with your side effects. Try not to stand by. Being proactive is significant so you can perhaps stop the descending slide sooner. It's simpler to move out of a shallow opening than the one you have been gradually digging and burrowing into for quite some time."

Stress can result from numerous individual, proficient, and ecological causes. The most effective way to adapt to stress is by dealing with the stressors inside your control. For instance, you could leave poisonous connections or leave stressful work. Likewise, you can work on tolerating or adapting to the stressors beyond your control with activities like reflecting or drinking less caffeine and liquor.

Depression can make it substantially harder to control or adapt to stressors. However, searching out directing or treatment or taking drugs can permit you to face stressors and manage them positively and helpfully more readily.

Negative emotions are terrible and troublesome close-to-home responses. Instances of negative emotions include misery, dread, outrage, or envy. These sentiments aren't simply unsavory; they make it hard to work in your typical routine and disrupt your capacity to achieve objectives.

It is vital to note that no inclination is intrinsically terrible, including a negative one. Feeling these things in specific settings or situations is entirely typical. When these emotions are steady and slow down your capacity to carry on with your life regularly, they become dangerous.

Everybody feels negative emotions occasionally, yet at times, these sentiments may indicate a psychological wellness condition like depression or tension.

TYPES OF NEGATIVE EMOTIONS

Various sentiments are much of the time distinguished as negative emotions. While such sentiments are often a typical response to specific encounters or events, these sentiments will generally be distressing and upsetting. A few normal sorts of negative emotions include:

- Outrage
- Uneasiness or dread
- Indifference
- Hatred, disdain, or loathing
- Envy
- Instability
- Lament or culpability
- Misery, sadness, or depression
- Disgrace

Negative emotions can come from a wide assortment of sources. At times they are the aftereffect of explicit encounters or events. For instance, you could feel upset that your #1 group didn't dominate a match or enraged that your accomplice was late for a booked date.

HOWEVER, NEGATIVE EMOTIONS CAN ALSO ARISE FROM:

RELATIONSHIP STRUGGLE: Issues that arise from relational connections are a typical reason for negative emotions. Such difficulties can arise in associations with companions, family, colleagues, or significant others.

NEGLECTED NEEDS: When your requirements are not being satisfied — whether these necessities are physical, emotional, social, mental, or profound — it is typical to encounter misery, outrage, forlornness, envy, and other distressing emotions.

POOR COPING SKILLS: Ordinary stress can prompt a wide assortment of disturbing sentiments if you don't have the coping skills to oversee it. Poor coping skills are not just a wasteful method for overseeing stress and negative emotions; they frequently wind up exacerbating the issue or acquainting new issues with the circumstance.

Negative emotions can be momentary responses to the occasions in your life, or they might come from other fundamental issues, including neglected needs, relationship issues, or poor coping skills.

UNHEALTHY WAYS OF COPING

Tragically, individuals frequently go to pointless or even damaging approaches to coping with negative emotions. A portion of these include:

DISREGARDING THE EMOTIONS: Overlooking sentiments (like "stuffing your resentment") isn't the best method for managing them. Taking everything into account doesn't cause them to vanish; however, it can make them come out unexpectedly. That is because your emotions signal that what you are doing in your life is or alternately isn't working.

RUMINATING ON THE INCLINATION: Rumination includes harping on outrage, hatred, and other awkward sentiments. It enhances negative emotions, yet it likewise brings well-being results. So it's fundamental to pay attention to your sentiments and afterward do whatever it may take to let them go.

WITHDRAWAL OR AVOIDANCE: When something is distressing, you could attempt to keep away from it so you don't need to encounter those disagreeable emotions. For instance, assuming something causes you nervousness, you could attempt to keep away from what is setting off those emotions. The issue is that this aversion to coping aggravates your negative emotions over the long term.

DESTRUCTIVE OR RISKY BEHAVIORS: While you are not managing the emotions you are feeling, they can create some issues with your physical and emotional wellbeing. It is especially obvious if you depend on dangerous ways of behaving, for example, substance use or self-damage, to adapt to distressing emotions.

Feeling furious or baffled can be a sign that something needs to change. If you don't change the circumstances or thought designs causing these awkward emotions, you will keep being set off by them.

HOW TO COPE WITH NEGATIVE EMOTIONS

Luckily, there are more useful ways of managing troublesome emotions. These systems can assist you with coping while additionally working on your capacity to direct your emotions.

UNDERSTAND YOUR EMOTIONS

Search inside and pinpoint the circumstances causing stress and negative emotions in your day-to-day existence. Taking a gander at the wellspring of the inclination and your response can give important data.

Negative emotions can emerge from setting off an occasion, like a staggering responsibility. Your contemplations encompassing an occasion likewise assume a part. How you decipher what happened can adjust how you experience the occasion and whether it causes stress.

A vital motivation behind your emotions is to inspire you to see the issue so that you can roll out important improvements.

CHANGE WHAT YOU CAN

When you better figure out your emotions and what is causing them, you can begin doing whatever it takes to resolve the issue. Limiting or wiping out a portion of your stress triggers might cause you to feel negative emotions less of the time.

SOME WAYS THAT YOU MIGHT ACCOMPLISH THIS INCLUDE

- Eliminating down on position stress, frequently by appointing errands, creating limits, and looking for help
- Learning the acts of decisive correspondence to oversee relationship clashes
- Changing negative idea designs through an interaction known as mental rebuilding

Few out of every odd wellspring of stress can be changed or killed. It is fundamental to abstain from ruminating about what you can't change and zero in on what's inside your control.

FIND AN OUTLET

Creating changes in your day-to-day existence can eliminate negative emotions; however, it will not dispose of your stress triggers. As you make changes in your day-to-day activities to achieve less dissatisfaction, you will likewise have to track down vital Sources for managing these emotions.

• Customary activity can give an emotional lift and a source for negative emotions.

• Reflection can assist you with discovering some internal "space" to work with so your emotions don't feel overpowering.

• Tracking down open doors for having a good time and getting more giggling in your life can significantly impact your viewpoint and ease stress.

Recollect that everybody's requirements and capacities are unique. The key is frequently to attempt a couple of different techniques to find what works for yourself and your circumstance. You'll feel less wrecked when negative emotions arise whenever you have found ideal procedures.

ACCEPT YOUR EMOTIONS

Figuring out how to acknowledge negative emotions is likewise a successful approach to dealing with these troublesome sentiments. Acknowledgment implies recognizing that we feel apprehensive, angry, miserable, or baffled. Rather than attempting to keep away from or stifle these sentiments, you permit them to exist without harping on them.

When you acknowledge your emotions, you quit attempting to limit or stifle them. All things being equal, you recognize they exist yet perceive that these sentiments are brief and can't hurt you.

HOW ACCEPTING EMOTIONS CAN IMPROVE YOUR HEALTH

Negative emotions will occur regardless of whether you generally have an uplifting perspective. Knowing how to deal with these reactions can assist you with feeling quite a bit improved at the time and what's in store.

Research has shown that strategies like stifling your emotions are insufficient and could be hurtful. So rather than attempting to overlook your sentiments, tracking down ways of understanding, acknowledging, and reexamining your emotions is often more supportive.

Negative emotions are typical and, surprisingly, anticipated. The objective isn't to curb these sentiments but to track down better management approaches. Building these coping skills can prompt more prominent emotional flexibility and prosperity.

Stress, dread, outrage, and misery are typical, sound emotions until they disrupt your capacity to do what you need or need to do. Numerous administration procedures can assist you with coping with your emotional stress. If you've attempted a few cures but feel overpowered or stuck, look for help from a guide or psychological wellness specialist.

WHAT IS EMOTIONAL STRESS?

Stress is an ordinary response to the tensions of daily existence. Stress, dread, outrage, trouble, and different emotions are all ordinary emotional reactions. They are all essential for life. Assuming the stress underlies these emotions impedes your capacity to do the things you need or have to do, this stress has become unfortunate.

WARNING SIGNS AND SYMPTOMS OF EMOTIONAL STRESS

Side effects of emotional stress can be both physical, mental, and social.

Physical symptoms include Weight in your chest, expanded pulse, or chest torment.

Shoulder, neck, or back torment; general body a throbbing painfulness.

Migraines.

Grating your teeth or holding your jaw.

Windedness.

Unsteadiness.

Feeling drained, restless, and discouraged.

You are losing or putting on Weight; changes in your dietary patterns.

I am resting pretty much more than expected.

Gastrointestinal issues include an annoyed stomach, loose bowels, or obstruction.

Sexual troubles.

Mental or social side effects include:

Being more emotional than expected.

You are feeling overpowered or tense.

Inconvenience monitoring things or recalling.

You are instigating choices, taking care of issues, concentrating, and finishing your work.

We are utilizing liquor or medications to ease your emotional stress.

HOW CAN I COPE BEST WITH EMOTIONAL STRESS

Numerous procedures can be attempted to assist you with better dealing with your emotional stress.

Carve out the opportunity to unwind: Set aside some margin to focus on yourself. Regardless of whether you can commit simply five to 15 minutes a couple of times each day to relax and enjoy some time off from the real world. What action assists you with unwinding? A few thoughts include:

READ A BOOK.

Download and pay attention to a "quiet" application (hints of nature, downpour) on your PC or telephone.

Go for a stroll—practice yoga.

Pay attention to music, chime into a tune, or dance to music.

Partake in a relieving shower.

Sit peacefully with your eyes shut.

Light a scented flame.

PRACTICE CARE: Care is figuring out how to concentrate and become more mindful. You can figure out how to feel the actual changes in your body that occur in light of your evolving emotions. Understanding this brain-body association is the initial phase in figuring out how to all the more likely deal with your stress and what emotions mean for your body. Care can likewise assist you with zeroing in your psyche on the quick - how might I carry my brain and body to a position of tranquility. If you can sort out what assists you with feeling more cool-headed at that time, you realize you've sorted out one of your stress triggers and what attempts to oversee it.

Occupy your brain and spotlight on something different:

Spotlight your psyche on some other options from what's causing your stress.

Accomplish something fun.

Watch an entertaining film, play a game, or participate in a most loved leisure activity (paint, draw, take pictures of nature, play with your pet).

Volunteer for an action to help other people.

Accomplish something with individuals you appreciate.

Have a go at journaling: Journaling is the practice of recording your thoughts and sentiments so you can comprehend them all the more plainly. It is a strategy that encourages you to dial back, focus, and ponder what is happening in your life - and your sentiments and responses to these happenings. Since journaling can uncover your deepest thoughts, it can uncover your emotional stress triggers. You can recognize and afterward supplant pessimistic thoughts and sentiments with ways of behaving that are more sure. Journaling is a solid and positive method for confronting your feelings. When you face your feelings, mending or change can start.

PRACTICE REFLECTION: Contemplation is one more approach to divert your thoughts effectively. By picking your thought process about, for example, positive thoughts or warm, consoling recollections, you can deal with your feelings and lessen your emotional stress.

WHEN TO GET HELP FOR EMOTIONAL STRESS

If you have any of the side effects of emotional stress, attempted at least one of the cures discussed in this section, and haven't tracked down alleviation, look for proficient assistance. If you feel overpowered and can't deal with your feelings and stresses all alone, look for the assistance of an expert. Try not to remain "frozen" or feel like you're pausing your breathing trusting that your sentiments will be finished. If you are trapped in a hopeless cycle and can't get yourself out, look for proficient assistance.

MASTERING SURVIVAL SKILLS IN THE WILDERNESS

Mastering survival skills in your backyard is a protected and simple method for setting yourself up before going wild. The following are eight fundamental skills to acquire and dominate so you are prepared to handle any survival situation.

1. BUILDING A FIRE

Fire can keep you warm, deflect trackers, and intensify cooking. Building a fire can be more earnestly than it looks, particularly if the weather conditions are sodden or cloudy or in a survival situation when you have few or no provisions.

There are a few imaginative ways to make fire with no stuff, yet they require practice and tolerance. Testing a couple of fire-building skills in your backyard is a great method for getting ready for a crisis.

Practice finding or making dry kindling via cutting a plume stick or chasing after amadou, a parasite that fills in the bark of coniferous trees. You can likewise dig around your backyard for quartz to create a stone that can produce a flash.

2. CREATING POTABLE WATER

Obtaining clean drinking water may be the most significant expertise required in a survival situation. Sadly, regular water sources are not generally clean and can hold onto parasites, infections, and microscopic organisms. You can create consumable water in the wild with two or three clear methods that you can without a doubt practice at home.

The most straightforward method for purging water in the wild is to bubble it; however, you might be left with silt or other particulate matter that influences the taste. You can try using a T-shirt or inside a bottle, insert sand and small river rocks to filter the water.

If you can't find a wellspring of water, you can practice drawing water from the Earth by still building a sunlight-based. A sun-oriented still comprises an opening roughly two feet across by one foot down. Place a compartment at the base and cover the opening with a canvas or plastic sheet, fixing the edges with soil or sand. Place a little stone in the focal point of the cover, and dampness will gather on the underside of the cover and tear into the compartment.

3. FORAGING FOR FOOD

The number of palatable wild plants accessible in your backyard ranch or around your area is amazing. In a survival situation, plants are a fundamental wellspring of supplements that can give a low-influence wellspring of energy.

Distinguishing eatable plants can be precarious, as numerous harmful species are comparable to non-poisonous ones. Yet, a couple of effectively recognizable plants developing the nation wildly over are supplement thick and delectable, including stinging bramble, dandelion, sheep's quarters, and excavator's lettuce.

If you are unpracticed at scavenging for food, it is ideal for keeping away from organisms and mushrooms, as numerous species are destructive. You can similarly search for a method for working on your ID methods in your backyard by counseling a neighborhood herbal manual.

4. TYING KNOTS

A frequently ignored expertise, tie tying can assist your possibilities of survival by assisting you with building a sanctuary, putting out traps, and making instruments. Figuring out how to tie secure bunches takes time and practice, so get a rope and hopefully look for a way to improve your bunch tying skills.

5. MAKING A WEAPON

You have little protection against hunters searching for a simple supper if you wind up in the wild without a weapon. A slingshot is an underestimated instrument that is speedy and simple to make from fundamental materials you can find at home. All you want is a forked stick, elastic tubing, and calfskin or material for the cushion.

Set up two or three concentrations around your yard whenever you have developed your slingshot, and practice picking up and firing away. Wear eye security and assurance that no one enters your view as you release your ammo.

6. BUILDING A SHELTER

Looking for cover is possibly the earliest errand to achieve on the off chance that you lose all sense of direction in the wild; however, a protected spot to keep out of the components can be elusive. Set out to utilize your young life stronghold-building skills and practice developing a stopgap cover in your backyard.

Dependent upon the scene, environment, and season, there are a couple of decisions for covers that you would be able to construct. Begin with an essential shelter or canvas tent, and step by step, develop your skills until you are open to lashing together lengthy branches to frame a teepee. If you live in a space with weighty winter snows, you can make the most of the chilly climate to practice digging a snow cave cover.

7. BASIC FIRST AID

At some point, when you're out in the wild, it might be hard for emergency organizations to reach you, assuming that you are cleared out or hurt. Understanding and choosing to oversee a clinical guide might save your life or the existence of somebody you love.

Get a companion, accomplice, or relative and practice regulating emergency treatment for a progression of normal dangers in survival situations. These incorporate the essential CPR methodology, control dying, treat consumption, balance out appendages, and alleviate plants for bug stings and scraped spots.

Laying out a trap to get a little game and survival fishing are fundamental skills that permit you to get significant wellsprings of protein with little energy consumption. Catches and fishing procedures change, contingent upon your prey, so it is critical to practice setting a wide range of catches and sending a scope of fishing strategies. Hence, you are ready for any situation.

Assuming that you practice laying out traps in your backyard, ensure you dismantle them after you are finished to try not to harm nearby natural life or neighborhood pets.

THE TAKEAWAY

Do whatever it takes not to hang on until you are adhered to in the wild to practice your survival skills. Mastering fundamental skills, for example, fire fabricating and building a haven, is an extraordinary end-of-the-week project you can do in the security of your backyard.

BOOK 12: A USEFUL LIST OF GOOD BUNKERS AND PLACES IN CASE OF WW3: SO YOU CAN BE READY WHEN THINGS GO WRONG

World War 3 is a situation nobody needs to work out as expected. Fortunately, there are no indications of it breaking out unavoidably. Yet, with the surprise spreading out in the world, we're finding out increasingly more about the significance of being ready. It turns out that a few nations are more ready than others.

With the world on hold of an extraordinary pandemic, the truth that the surprising can happen has never been more present. Consistently, the world becomes more aware of the significance of being ready and secured. However, nothing remains to be said a third World War could break out; a few objections are ready for atomic warfare.

Although many bunkers stay covered up and secret, a couple of present-day safe-houses are known to people.

A bunker will, in general, be a construction incorporated low into the ground - an entire underground hideout fit for safeguarding its occupants for a while, ideally lengthy enough to shield from the tricky times over the ground.

Most nations don't presently have Judgment day bunkers set up for their residents, yet certain individuals have assumed control over planning.

USA

However, the American government has not constructed a progression of bunkers; some in the country have utilized their money to get ready for the direst outcome imaginable.

In 2008 a mogul, Larry Hall, bought a resigned rocket storehouse in Savannah, Georgia, and changed it into an underground townhouse for the super-rich.

Metro reports that it is just one of its sort in the USA.

The underground structure is named "endurance condominium." As indicated by its site, "it offers individual responsibility for the private unit inside a superstructure that offers the most elevated level of actual insurance, the excess foundation for power, water, air, and food, and "shared or normal" offices; for stretched out off-lattice endurance." Mr. Hall, the task chief, and proprietor, says: "This venture enjoys the benefits of allowing the individuals to claim a piece of history, the coolness of a rocket base, the security of an atomic solidified bunker, and the highlights of an extravagance townhouse."

A half-floor unit is valued at $1,500,000 (£1,210,477), in the mean time a full-floor suite goes for around $3,000,000 (£2,42,0955).

Not exclusively is each hideout suite kitted out with every one of the conveniences of a very good quality condo. The complex likewise flaunts its indoor pool, practice office, rock climbing divider, cinema, arcade, and, surprisingly, a canine park.

MOLDOVA

Secret in the previous Soviet territory of Moldova are two bunkers that were found to prompt a whole underground city purportedly worked for high positioning officials should a third World War break out.

Known to the British and US spies as "Article 1180," these two designs were worked in 1985 - at the level of the Cold War.

Safeguarded inside the thick dividers is an entire world underneath the ground, including shops, emergency clinics, and a tremendous measure of provisions.

As per YouTube star Benjamin Rich, who now and again investigates the locale: "The Soviet Union worked around four of these monster atomic bunkers specked around the previous country for the central leadership to stow away in and order the powers ought to, seemingly the unavoidable, occur.

"They began development in 1985; however, as the Soviet Empire reached a conclusion, there was no requirement for [them] any longer."

NEW ZEALAND

Seven Silicon Valley wealthy people were accounted for to have gobbled up land in New Zealand last year. Would it be a good idea for them if they needed to escape the US during a worldwide emergency?

The gathering constructed homes in the nation, complete with secret 150-ton atomic bunkers 13 feet beneath the ground.

The bunkers were worked by Texas-based bunker maker Rising S Company, whose extreme underground hideout named "The Aristocrat" comes in at an astounding £8.9million, barring the establishment charge.

It has a limit concerning over 50 individuals in differing levels of extravagance and highlights impenetrable entryways, a sun-oriented produced charging framework, a pool, a bowling path, and a weapon range, among different extravagances.

Nonetheless, there are a few nations where confidential underground bunkers aren't required.

ALBANIA

As per the BBC, Albania is the farmhouse with the most underground bunkers, with around 1,000,000 specked all through the country.

These substantial designs were worked during the dubious long periods of the cold war, between the 1960s and 1980s, under the socialist government of Enver Hoxha.

There are presently 5.7 bunkers for each square kilometer of land. In any case, the good news is they never must be utilized for their planned reason.

Built from cement, steel, and iron, the bunkers range in size from a couple of individual pillboxes with space for weapons to colossal underground sanctuaries used to stow away enormous gatherings.

As of late, with little requirement for the bunkers, many have been changed into eateries and restaurants.

Notwithstanding, some stay, prepared for local people to escape into should the most exceedingly terrible become a reality.

UK

YORK

York isn't just a dazzling city in that frame of mind of Yorkshire however is home to a Cold War bunker.

The bunker was dynamic from the 1960s until the 1990s and was utilized to screen the aftermath in case of an atomic assault.

It is not normal for some other cities in the UK with a rich Roman and Viking past and encompassed by the Yorkshire Dales, North York Moors, and WoldsUK.

The Cold War bunker contains an air filtration framework and producing plant, a kitchen and feline nee, dorms, radio and landline correspondence gear, and expert 1980s PCs.

The bunker is currently an English Heritage Scheduled Monument and can be visited.

LONDON

Although London isn't known for being essentially protected, it is home to the Kingsway phone trade-in Holborn.

Situated in the core of focal London close to Chancery Lane, this Cold War-time bargain-level bargain-level air strike safe house could be ideal for getting away from World War 3.

Albeit expected to be utilized as a sanctuary, it was rather utilized as a government interchanges focus.

The haven is only a short distance from St Paul's, Covent Garden, Leicester Square, and plenty of London's best attractions.

CHESHIRE

Cheshire isn't known for being especially touristy however is home to a few shocking sights.

Arley Hall and Gardens, Beeston Castle, and the shocking Chester Cathedral are only a portion of the district's sights.

However, Cheshire is likewise home to Hack Green Secret Nuclear Bunker, a government-possessed atomic bunker.

The Home Office took over the, yet in 1992, toward the finish of the Cold War, it was deserted and bought by a privately owned business.

It is presently open to the general population to visit with an assortment of military and Cold War memorabilia.

The town of Kidderminster is a noteworthy market town in Worcestershire that is only 17 miles from the clamoring city of Birmingham.

Likewise, the town is home to the Drakelow Tunnels, a previous underground military complex under Blakeshall Estate only north of the pleasant town.

However, they were worked during World War 2 and were created during the Cold War.

The passages, as of now, stay unused.

WHERE TO GO FOR HELP IN CASE OF A WW3

A great deal is changing in our reality, and numerous people appear to be stressing over an impending WW3.

However, what might be said about if you would move to an unfamiliar place of refuge, couldn't unreasonably be exquisite?

Coincidentally there are a few areas where you'd have a very good potential for success in enduring the apocalypse. Would it be a good idea for everything to go to Pete Tong?

From the frozen deserts of Iceland to the developed city of Cape Town, these spots are great for enduring any hopeless situation that what's to come holds.

THESE ARE NINE PLACES TO BE IF EVERYTHING GETS DOWNRIGHT UGLY.

ICELAND

As Insider reports, Iceland is many miles from some other land, so it ought not to be an objective in a World War 3 situation.

Furthermore, it's an incredible spot for fishing, so survivors would have a bountiful food supply to push them along until the world is reconstructed.

ISLE OF LEWIS

This Scottish island is independent and arranged three hours from the central area.

It's a sufficiently pleasant spot to live without drawing any regard for yourself.

ANTARCTICA

It very well might be a piece nippy. Yet, in the worst situation imaginable, you'd presumably be protected if you figured out how to cut out a day-to-day existence in the mainland's desolate waste.

KANSAS CITY

In the case of a non-atomic war, this is the spot to be. The city is encircled by prolific farmland and is the best spot to protect against assailants.

YUKON

One of Canada's most far-off areas, the Yukon region, is wealthy in the framework.

To make matters far superior, it's a mineral-rich region jam-loaded with untamed life, meaning you could get rich and eat well while trusting that the end times will blow over.

CAPE TOWN

South Africa's richest city, Cape Town, could be a good spot to hang out in solace.

Since the African country keeps itself generally clear of Western impacts, there's a good opportunity that Cape Town will be such a long way far removed that World War 3 won't arrive at it.

GUAM

Guam is a wise spot to take cover to endure a worldwide struggle and an effectively defendable island with a solid military presence.

BERN

Switzerland doesn't favor one side, preferring to remain neutral through each major conflict.

Furthermore, Bern, the Swiss capital, is effectively solid for sure, not that war is probably going to come to Switzerland.

TRISTAN DA CUNHA

This assortment of islands is probably the remotest put on Earth and is a top fishing spot.

We can imagine far more terrible spots to spend the apocalypse than on staggering island heaven in no place.

BOOK 13: A READY-MADE SHOPPING LIST TELLS YOU WHAT FOOD TO BUY AND IN WHAT QUANTITIES TO SURVIVE FOR AN ENTIRE YEAR WITHOUT GOING TO THE STORE

WHY STORE A YEAR'S WORTH OF FOOD

Everybody has reasons for choosing to stock their pantries for a lengthy timeframe. If you are still going back and forth about why you truly need to start storing food long-term, the following are a couple of reasons to assist you with choosing.

Save Time - Storing food, whether for seven days, a month, or a year, will save you time over the long term. Having food stored available will limit the time you spend at stores and, in some cases, limit the time it takes to plan meals.

Save Money: When you purchase items in mass, you are saving cash because, most times, the cost per unit is lower than when purchased separately. Developing your produce can save cash; you are paying for the cost of seeds or transplants.

Emergencies: Emergencies can be cataclysmic events, a pandemic, the cutback of employment, or a significant physical issue. Numerous things can fall into this class. Having your food stored for long means that you will have less stress when something like this occurs.

Natural Friendly - Buying things in mass and preserving uses less bundling and causes less waste. Canning jars can be used repeatedly, and there are currently reusable top alternatives.

COOKING WITH SALT, SALT QUESTIONS

We purchase Redmond's Fine Sea Salt in a 25-pound pack. It's less expensive to purchase in mass, and we use it for numerous such things (maturing, preserving, and from-scratch meals) that it seemed OK to get an enormous sack.

WHERE TO START WHEN STORING A YEAR'S WORTH OF FOOD

Assuming you have chosen to assume command over your food security and might need to endeavor to store long-term, my best exhortation is to start small. Many tragically bounce in both feet first about long-term food storage, and afterward, they end up wrecked with food waste.

TIPS BEFORE YOU START STORING FOOD:

Try not to take a stab at storing a whole year's worth of food from scratch. Start small: plan for the multi-month storage and work from that point afterward.

Monitor your inventory and storage space.

Purchasing in mass can save you time and cash.

Store a couple of key ingredients in mass, and afterward, continue toward an alternate one.

If you have never preserved your food, ease into it. Try not to rely upon home-preserved food altogether until you have taken in the ins and outs.

Assuming that purchasing fresh produce in mass, purchase in-season to assist with diminishing the cost.

Have a Plan! Sort out what food you will store, the amount you will need, and how you will store it.

Step-by-step instructions to Store a Year's Worth of Food for Your Family (Without Waste and Overwhelm)

It took me a couple of years to arrive at this point: making a feast for supper made from food made solely on our homestead.

HOW TO BUILD A CUSTOMIZED PLAN TO STORE A YEAR'S WORTH OF FOOD

You should start with an arrangement before you hop in and start purchasing or preserving your storage items. This plan will assist you with getting coordinated and forestall overpowering. Snatch a pencil and some paper, carve out an opportunity to work everything out (or look at the final pages from my Old-Fashioned on Purpose Planner).

CREATING YOUR CUSTOMIZED FOOD STORAGE PLAN

(1) SET REALISTIC, ACTIONABLE GOALS

Any well-thought-out plan starts with setting goals and having an unmistakable thought of what you would like the result to be. Start by recording your short-term goals, long-term goals, and what is persuading you to make a move.

(2) WRITE DOWN WHAT YOUR FAMILY EATS

Sort out what recipes and foods your family uses most and focus on these. The objective is to reserve what your family will eat.

(3) CHECK THE STORAGE SPACE YOU HAVE

You need to store a year's worth of food, yet you should consider how much storage space you have and where you can make more if necessary.

(4) WHAT DOES YOUR INVENTORY LOOK LIKE

Commence your food storage process by going through your storeroom, cooler, and root basement (assuming you are adequately fortunate to have one) to see what you have close by. You will need to take everything out, go through what you use, and what you can dispose of.

Note: Organize your Pantry/Freezer, and afterward, make an inventory sheet to monitor what you have and what you want. It doesn't need to be extravagant; just a piece of lined paper will do.

(5) STORE-BOUGHT, HOMEGROWN, OR BOTH

During the arranging stage, you should choose if you will be developing products, raising meat, preserving yourself, or purchasing everything. You can do everything for a couple. If you can raise chickens yet are set on fresh ranch produce, you can go to a farmers' market. Numerous combinations and options for customizing your arrangement to accommodate your situation are significant.

ORGANIZING AND CREATING YOUR LONG-TERM STORAGE SPACE

Before you stress over what and the amount to store, you should be sure that you have the space to store your food long-term. During your arranging, a list of storage space and existing inventory should have been made; presently, the time has come to clean and sort these spaces.

Note: It doesn't need to be an ordinary attempt to use what you have and get inventive when it comes to storage space.

There is a wide range of places you can store your food items, so consider the accompanying spaces while concluding the amount of space you possess to store a year's worth of food.

DIFFERENT STORAGE SPACE IDEAS TO CONSIDER:

- Cupboards
- Storage space/Larder
- Root Cellar
- Closets
- Basements
- Additional Refrigerator
- Cooler
- Outbuildings

You also can sort out your bigger storage areas by separating them using smaller containers. Something essential to recall is to name your containers so there is no confusion later on.

CONTAINERS TO HELP ORGANIZE YOUR STORAGE SPACE:

- Baskets
- Crates
- Totes
- Boxes
- Shelves
- Glass Jars
- Food Grade Buckets

Whenever you have sorted out precisely the amount of space you possess for storage, the time has come to sort out how much food your family should store. Can your storage space hold how much food is required? How about we find out!

One of the significant mistakes individuals make in storing food long-term is stocking up on durable items disregarding what will get eaten. As referenced before, you genuinely must focus on storing things that your family will eat because this will forestall food waste from here on out.

In your arrangement (referenced above), you recorded your most-loved recipes and glanced at foods your family consistently consumes. Presently, you need to separate these recipes into basic fixing lists, so later, you will know what to incorporate while purchasing or preserving.

On the off chance that you are purchasing most of your stocked food, you need to focus on things that have a long shelf life, like canned goods, pasta, rice, and dried beans. Nobody wants to stock up on something then, at that point, figure out it has spoiled in a short time.

STORE A YEAR'S WORTH OF FOOD

LONG-TERM FOOD STORAGE ITEMS ARE AS FOLLOWS:

- Grains
- Oats
- Rice
- Dry Beans
- Pasta
- Canned or Frozen Vegetables
- Canned Sauces
- Got dried out Fruits

- Dried Herbs
- Nuts
- Peanut Butter
- Honey
- Salt
- Fats and Oils
- Canned or Frozen Meats

STEP-BY-STEP INSTRUCTIONS TO STORE A YEAR'S WORTH OF FOOD FOR YOUR FAMILY (WITHOUT WASTE AND OVERWHELM)

HOW MUCH SHOULD TO STORE FOR A YEAR'S WORTH OF FOOD

There are various methods and calculators that can assist you with drawing near to an estimated sum to store for a year's worth of food. These can help; however, there is nobody size-fits-all solution, so you should adjust to customize the sum for your situation. For instance, assuming you have developing kids, they might eat enough for two individuals contrasted with their 40-year-old mother.

Different Things to Factor in When Deciding Your Amounts:

SEASONS - One thing that sometimes gets neglected is the seasons. For instance, if you eat vegetables with each feast, you could require canned vegetables while fresh produce isn't accessible.

AGE - Remember to consider the time of everybody in your family while customizing your amounts.

WELLBEING: Health can be another determining factor regarding the sum someone will eat.

OTHER THINGS TO CONSIDER WHEN DECIDING YOUR AMOUNTS:

TECHNIQUE 1: FAVORITE RECIPE BREAKDOWN

Separate your recipe into basic ingredients, and afterward, increase these by 12; presently, you know the amount to store if you eat this once a month of the year. Whenever you have stored that one recipe, you can continue to the following and go on until your schedule is loaded up with meals.

How you separate your recipes relies heavily on how fundamental you might need to get with your fixings. If you make all that without any preparation, your rundown will incorporate more things.

HERE IS AN ILLUSTRATION FOR SPAGHETTI NIGHT

1 - 16oz Boxes of Noodles x 12 = 12 Boxes of Spaghetti Noodles

1 - Container of Spaghetti Sauce x 12 = 12 Containers of Spaghetti

1 lb - 1 Ground Beef x12 = 12 lbs Ground Beef

1 - Loaf of French Bread x 12 = 12 Portions of Bread

Note: This model is for a fundamental locally acquired spaghetti supper; with time and experience, you can break this down further into the essential homemade renditions (like homemade pasta and homemade French bread)

TECHNIQUE 2: FOOD PER INDIVIDUAL EACH DAY

Work out how much and what every relative typically eats each day, then duplicate these discoveries by seven, and you currently have a thought of how much is consumed in a multi-week. Go through your multi-week and work to multi-month, and afterward a year.

TECHNIQUE 3: BATCH COOKING

Cluster cooking is one of my number one methods for putting away food and saving time. Assuming that you anticipate making vegetable soup for supper one evening, simply make extra, and afterward either can or freeze the additional soup for meals on various evenings. You will most likely be unable to bunch cook for a whole year, yet if you keep doing that for a period, you can move toward it.

Utilizing group cooking for your drawn-out storage framework again expects that you separate your recipes into the fundamental fixings and duplicate how much every fixing by the sum you are making.

Example: Vegetable Soup Fixings x 4 = 4 Suppers = 1 Vegetable Soup Supper each 4 months

HOW TO BUILD YOUR FOOD STORAGE

Since last year's flour storage, I purchase wheat berries in mass and crush them into flour at whatever point I want it.

INSTRUCTIONS TO ASSEMBLE YOUR FOOD STORAGE

TIP 1: PURCHASE MORE AT A TIME

At the start of your food storage mission, purchasing really in mass can be a battle. There are ways you can approach purchasing extra as you go. My number 1 tip: Spotlight on one item and begin purchasing extra every time you are at the store to develop stock and continue to another.

You can likewise zero in on one recipe that your family appreciates and purchase your elements for it, and when you have your limited sum, continue toward the following one. This method can be gone on until you have all your ideal suppers.

TIP 2: PURCHASE IN MASS

Become an individual from an enormous store like Costco, where most of the things you will be searching for will be sold in mass. When you purchase your things in mass, this will save you both time and cash.

TIP 3: BECOME YOUR OWN/LOCAL

Assuming it's feasible for you, develop your food, including produce, meat, eggs, honey, or anything you are creating yourself. At times you have the opportunity and space; you can grow a year of production to protect. Save chickens for meat and eggs, or perhaps some time or another stir up to purchasing and raising a pig (see how to sort out the expense of raising your meat here).

Developing your product and raising your meat is extraordinary because you know precisely where your food supply is coming from.

Assuming you have your heart set on developing your product, you should consider:

- Your Developing Space
- Developing Zone/Environment
- What Vegetables Your Family Needs
- The number of Plants that are Required

While developing your product, you should sort out the number of plants you should plant to have the option to save a year's worth. If you are a cultivating and safeguarding novice, it may be more straightforward to zero in on one yield beginning.

Tomatoes are typically a go-to model since it is a particularly flexible organic product in a wide range of recipes; you have your pureed tomatoes, tomato glue, pizza sauce, and, surprisingly, sun-dried tomatoes, to give some examples. To get an adequate number of tomatoes for any of these tomato items, you will require 3-5 plants for every individual.

To get a superior clarification, watch my video Realize Precisely The amount to Plant to Take care of Your Family, where I talk you through a situation that assists me with sorting out the amount to plant.

TIP 4: SAFEGUARD YOUR STORAGE THINGS

Safeguarding your food doesn't be guaranteed to mean developing your food, even though they do remain closely connected. You can get it from rancher's business sectors, side-of-the-road stands, or a neighborhood maker to save your merchandise.

If you have chosen to bring the jump into home safeguarding, you ought to realize that there are various methods. You can utilize only one method or a blend of them, anything that will make things simpler for you over the long term.

PRESERVATION METHODS TO CHOOSE FROM:

(1) CANNING

The Canning safeguarding method is one of the most utilized for long-term storage. Contingent upon what you need to store, you might boil water at any point, shower (figure out how to water shower can), or strain can make your things. Some decisions ought to be followed, and canning security should never be messed with.

(2) FREEZING

Freezing functions admirably for particular sorts of vegetables and most meats; the destruction to freezing is that in a crisis where power is lost, your cooler won't work. Likewise, it is a method that might require some whitening before your things get moved to the cooler.

(3) ROOT CELLARING/COLD STORAGE

This sort of storage isn't for a wide range of products, and it is utilized for winter squash, carrots, potatoes, beets, and different vegetables that like to be kept cool and in obscurity. You don't just have a genuine root basement to store things along these lines, yet it makes a difference.

(4) GETTING DRIED OUT

The getting dried out method is when you utilize a dehydrator or stove to eliminate the dampness from the picked food. Foods that are dried out can be incredible options for soups because many can be reestablished by adding water. Dried-tried-out foods don't occupy as much room as other protected foods, which can help if you don't have a lot of long-term storage space.

(5) MATURATION

This protection method has been utilized for a long time, and because of the salty salt water utilized, it is one of the most secure. Maturation is likewise an exceptionally essential method of safeguarding; just salt, vegetables, and a container are required.

Never saved anything? That is alright; find out about every method and how to protect your reap here.

ARE YOU SET NOW TO START STORING A YEAR'S WORTH OF FOOD FOR YOUR FAMILY?

The thought is to attempt to store to the point of helping you through one year; assuming you are new to food storage, simply recollect that the most effective way to forestall dissatisfaction and waste is to begin from the least. Make a modified arrangement that turns out best for your family and choose what you should purchase or create yourself.

I trust your food storage venture is fruitful and that you can assume command over your food supply. It is an extraordinary and fulfilling feeling to be independent and ready.

Like canned products and dried organic products, durable foods have a long period of usability and don't expect refrigeration to hold them back from spoiling. They can be put away at room temperature, like in a storage space or bureau.

They're standard kitchen things and are preferred by explorers and campers who can't bring transitory foods like new meats, dairy, and vegetables on the path.

Likewise, durable merchandise is fundamental in crisis circumstances and inclined toward beneficent associations that feed or give food to individuals confronting vagrancy or food frailty.

Albeit a few things like boxed macaroni and cheddar are loaded with additives and other undesirable fixings, many nutritious durable foods are accessible.

THE FOLLOWING ARE 12 OF THE BEST DURABLE FOODS WITH ALL THE INFORMATION YOU NEED ABOUT THEM.

1. DRIED AND CANNED BEANS

Dried and canned beans are shrewd durable food decisions with a long timeframe of realistic usability and high supplement content. Canned beans can be reserved at room temperature for 2-5 years, while dried beans can endure at least ten years, contingent upon the bundling.

One investigation discovered that pinto beans stockpiled for 30 years were viewed as consumable by 80% of individuals on a crisis food use board.

Beans are a great wellspring of fiber, plant-based protein, magnesium, B nutrients, manganese, iron, phosphorus, zinc, and copper. Also, they pair well with most foods and make generous augmentations to soups, grain dishes, and mixed greens.

2. NUT MARGARINE

Nut margarine is velvety, supplement thick, and tasty.

Although capacity temperatures can influence shelf life, business peanut butter saves for as long as nine months at room temperature. Regular peanut butter, which doesn't contain additives, endures as long as 90 days at 50°F (10°C) and just multi-month at 77°F (25°C).

As indicated by the US Division of Horticulture (USDA), almond spread saves for one year at room temperature, while cashew margarine keeps as long as 90 days.

Nut spreads are a rich wellspring of solid fats, protein, nutrients, minerals, and strong plant compounds, including phenolic cell reinforcements, which are intensified that safeguard your body against oxidative pressure and harm by unsteady particles called free revolutionaries.

Containers of nut spread can be put away in your storage space, while more modest parcels can be taken hiking or setting up camp for a nibble in a hurry.

3. DRIED FRUITS AND VEGETABLES

Albeit most new fruits and vegetables have a short shelf life, dried produce is viewed as durable. When appropriately put away, most dried natural products can be securely kept at room temperature for one year, and dried vegetables can be kept for around 50%.

You can browse an assortment of dried fruits and vegetables, including dried berries, apples, tomatoes, and carrots. Likewise, you can utilize a dehydrator or broiler to make your own dried fruits and vegetables. Vacuum-fixed bundling can assist with forestalling waste.

Dried fruits and veggies can be delighted in as a bite or added to a trail blend. Furthermore, dried veggies can be rehydrated by adding them to soups or stews if a new product isn't accessible.

4. CANNED FISH AND POULTRY

Albeit new fish and poultry are loaded with supplements, they're profoundly transient. No different either way; canned assortments can be securely saved without refrigeration for significant stretches — as long as five years at room temperature.

Fish and other fish items are additionally sold in lightweight bundles known as counter pockets, ideally suited for more modest storerooms and hiking. Fish in counter pockets has a shelf life of as long as a year and a half.

Chicken and different meats can also be found in answer pockets; however, you should refer to the shelf-life data bundling.

5. NUTS AND SEEDS

Nuts and seeds are compact, supplement thick, and shelf-stable, making them durable food staples. They're also perfect to have close, leaning toward explorers and climbers for fatty nibbling.

By and large, nuts last around four months when kept at or close to room temperature (68°F or 20°C); however, shelf life differs incredibly between nut assortments.

For instance, cashews can be saved for quite some time at 68°F (20°C) while pistachios, just a most recent multi-month at a similar temperature.

Seeds have equivalent shelf lives. As indicated by the USDA, pumpkin seeds stay new at room temperature for a very long time.

6. GRAINS

Entire grains like oats, rice, and grain have a significantly longer shelf life than other well-known; however, short-lived carb sources like bread are a brilliant decision for long-term food capacity.

For instance, earthy-colored rice can be kept at 50-70°F (10-21°C) for as long as 90 days, while farro endures as long as six months at room temperature.

Grains can be added to soups, mixed greens, and dishes, making them a flexible, durable fixing. In addition, eating entire grains might lessen your gamble of type 2 diabetes, coronary illness, and certain tumors.

7. CANNED VEGETABLES AND FRUITS

Canning has for quite some time been utilized to protract the shelf life of transient food sources, including fruits and vegetables.

The intensity utilized during canning kills possibly hurtful microorganisms, and the trademark mark of canned food sources holds new microscopic organisms back from spoiling the items.

The shelf lifespan of canned fruits and vegetables relies upon the kind of produce.

For instance, low-corrosive canned vegetables, including potatoes, carrots, beets, and spinach, last 2-5 years at room temperature.

Then again, high-corrosive fruits like grapefruit, apples, peaches, berries, and pineapple last only 12-year and a half. The equivalent goes for vegetables pressed in vinegar, like sauerkraut, German potato salad, and other cured vegetables.

While shopping, pick canned fruits pressed in water or 100 percent natural product squeeze instead of weighty syrup and decide on low sodium canned veggies whenever possible.

If you're sly in the kitchen, consider canning at home utilizing locally acquired or garden-developed vegetables and fruits if you don't have the foggiest idea of how you can counsel various books or online instructional exercises.

8. JERKY

Meat protection is a training utilized to keep protein sources from spoiling. In particular, jerky is made by relieving meat in a salt arrangement, then getting dried out. Additives, flavorings, and different added substances are utilized during handling.

Many jerkies are accessible, including meat, salmon, chicken, and bison. Even plant-based jerky choices are produced using coconut, banana, and jackfruit. Note that these options are not healthfully comparable to meat-based jerkies.

Business jerky can be securely saved in the storage space for one year; however, the USDA suggests that hand-crafted jerky be put away at room temperature for two months.

Any jerky can be appreciated with some restraint, yet the best choices are those that don't contain added sugar, fake flavors, or additives.

9. GRANOLA AND PROTEIN BARS

Granola and protein bars are the go-to nourishment for explorers and climbers because of their long shelf life and supplement synthesis.

Numerous granola bars stay new for one year at room temperature. Moreover, most protein bars have a shelf life of one year; however, checking the name on individual items for lapse information is ideal.

Additionally, granola and protein bars can be exceptionally nutritious the same length as you pick the right sorts. Search for brands loaded with generous fixings, like oats, nuts, and dried natural products, and contain negligible added sugars and fake fixings.

10. SOUP

Canned and dried soups are a magnificent decision while loading your storage room. Food gift associations likewise like them.

Most canned soups are low in corrosive and can endure as long as five years at room temperature. The special case is tomato-based assortments, which have a shelf life of around a year and a half.

Although most dried soup blends ought to endure as long as one year away, checking king names for lapse d is idealized.

Pick soups that are wealthy in solid fixings like vegetables and beans. Select low sodium items whenever the situation allows, as consuming an excess of added salt might hurt your wellbeing.

11. FREEZE-DRIED SUPPERS

Freeze drying utilizes sublimation, a cycle in which ice is changed over straightforwardly into fume, to eliminate water from food with the goal that it endures longer at room temperature. Freeze-dried dinners are famous among hikers because of their Light Weight and versatility.

Freeze-dried food varieties and prepared-to-eat freeze-dried suppers are made for long-term stockpiling — for certain items flaunting a 30-year taste.

Many organizations, including Wild Zora and AlpineAire, make tasty, freeze-dried suppers that are sound and oblige explicit dietary examples.

12. SHELF-STABLE MILK AND NON-DAIRY MILK

While new milk and some non-dairy choices like almond and coconut milk must be refrigerated, shelf-stable milk and numerous non-dairy milk are made to keep at room temperature.

Shelf-steady or aseptic milk is handled and bundled uniquely in contrast to normal milk since it's warmed to higher temperatures and pressed in sterile holders.

One investigation discovered that shelf-stable milk had a shelf life of nine months when kept at 40-68°F (4-20°C).

Plant-based drinks like soy milk bundled in adaptable materials, including plastic, paper, and aluminum, also last as long as ten months. In contrast, canned coconut milk lasts for five years at room temperature.

Shelf-stable and plant-based milk can be utilized when refrigeration isn't free. Powdered milk is a decent other option, with an expected shelf life of 3-5 years when kept in a cool, dull spot. It may be reconstituted with clean water in little parcels on a case-by-case basis.

THE MAIN CONCERN

Durable food varieties keep going for quite a while without spoiling and are essential for various circumstances.

Whether you need to give things to beneficent associations, get ready for expected crises, buy exploring cordial items, or just stock your storeroom, you can browse a wealth of quality food sources that don't need refrigeration.

After a Disaster

Remain calm and patient. Remaining composed and routine will help you move securely and stay away from postponements or mishaps brought about by nonsensical ways of behaving. Many individuals will be attempting to get precisely the same things done you are for their family's wellbeing. Tolerance will help everybody get past difficult circumstances without any problem.

Set your strategy in motion. Having specific strides to take will keep you pursuing your family's wellbeing.

Pay attention to neighborhood radio or TV for news and guidelines. Neighborhood specialists will give the most fitting counsel to your specific circumstance.

Check for wounds. Give medical aid and find support for genuinely harmed individuals. Dealing with yourself first will permit you to help others securely until crisis responders show up.

Help your neighbors who might need extraordinary support - newborn children, old endlessly individuals with handicaps - and individuals who care for them or huge families who might require extra help in a crisis circumstance.

Wear defensive apparel and rugged shoes. Disaster regions and garbage contain many dangers. The most widely recognized injury following disasters is cut feet.

Check for harm in your home. Disasters can cause broad harm, in some cases in places you least anticipate. Search cautiously for any possible perils.

Utilize battery-controlled lamps or spotlights while looking at structures. Battery-fueled lighting is the most secure and simplest and doesn't present a fire danger for the client, tenants, or building.

Try not to utilize candles. Candles can undoubtedly cause fires. They are calm, and it slipped effectively's minds. They can spill during tremor consequential convulsions or in a whirlwind. Candles welcome fire play by kids. Many individuals have passed on in private flames brought about by utilizing candles after a disaster than from the immediate effect of the actual disaster.

Search for fire dangers. There might be broken or spilling gas lines, overwhelmed electrical circuits, or lowered heaters or machines. Fire is the most continuous risk following floods.

Check for gas spills. Sniff for gas releases, beginning at the water radiator. If you smell gas or suspect a release, open a window and get everybody outside rapidly. Switch off the gas at the fundamental external valve if you can call the gas organization from a neighbor's home. If you switch off the gas under any condition, it should be walked out on by an expert.

Search for electrical framework harm. If you see ignites or broken or frayed wires, on the other hand, if you smell copying protection, switch off the power at the fundamental breaker box or electrical switch. If you need to step in water to get to the wire box or electrical switch, call an electrical expert first for counsel. Electrical gear should be checked and dried before being brought back to support.

Check for sewage and water lines harm. If you suspect sewage lines are harmed, try not to utilize the restrooms and call a handyperson. If water pipes are broken, contact the water organization and try not to use water from the tap. You can get protected water from flawless water radiators or softening ice shapes.

Tidy up spills right away. This incorporates prescriptions, dye, gasoline, and other combustible fluids.

Watch for free mortar and roofs that could fall.

Take photos of the harm, both the structure and its items, for protection claims.

Bind or secure your pets. They might be terrified and attempt to run.

Allow your family to know you have gotten back, and then, at that point, don't utilize the phone again unless it is a life-compromising crisis. Phone lines are regularly wrecked in disaster circumstances. They should be clear for emergency calls to get past.

Ensure you have a sufficient water supply if assistance is cut off. Water is much of the time tainted after serious disasters. An intact water warmer might be your best wellspring of drinking water.

Avoid falling down electrical cables and report them right away. Getting harmed utilities switched off will prevent further injury or harm. If conceivable, set out a flare and remain on the scene to caution others until specialists show up.

REFERENCES

https://www.mentalhelp.net/disasters/

https://emedicine.medscape.com/article/765495-overview

https://www.caloes.ca.gov/ICESite/pages/10-ways-to-be-prepared.aspx

https://ors.od.nih.gov/ser/dem/emergencyPrep/Pages/Disaster-Preparedness-Tips.aspx

https://edition.cnn.com/2019/07/12/us/how-to-prepare-for-natural-disasters-trnd/index.html

https://www.mercycorps.org/blog/7-ways-prepare-disaster

https://www.amazon.com/Off-Grid-Living-Collection-Gardening/dp/B092MLYJBW

https://offgridsurvival.com/preppersoffgrid/

https://www.epa.gov/sites/default/files/2015-03/documents/planning_for_an_emergency_drinking_water_supply.pdf

https://texashelp.tamu.edu/browse/disaster-preparedness-information/emergency-food-and-water-supplies/

https://www.iatp.org/documents/food-reserves-in-practice

https://www.webstaurantstore.com/article/454/types-of-cooking-methods.html

https://www.studential.com/university/student-cooking/cooking-methods

https://en.wikipedia.org/wiki/Home_medical_equipment

https://www.selfcarefederation.org/what-is-self-care

https://www.healthline.com/health/first-aid#Introduction-to-first-aid

https://www.webmd.com/first-aid/first-aid-kits-treatment

https://www.sciencedirect.com/

http://www.biecek.pl/statystykaMedyczna/Stevenson_survival_analysis_195.721.pdf

https://www.ready.gov/

https://dj.usembassy.gov/u-s-citizen-services/local-resources-of-u-s-citizens/emergency-preparedness/72-hour-kit/

https://www.who.int/publications/i/item/9789240003927?gclid=EAIaIQobChMI4vnBzKCk-AIVcIxoCR2f9AllEAAYASAAEgKaAfD_BwE

https://mental-health-survival-guide.com/

https://www.wikihow.com/Survive-a-War

https://www.loveproperty.com/

https://www.eatthis.com/write-effective-grocery-shopping-list/

https://food.unl.edu/article/basic-foods-checklist-how-stock-your-kitchen-simple-meals

Made in the USA
Las Vegas, NV
10 October 2022

56787098R00127